I0886960

Dossiers of Ancient Egyptians – the Middle Kingdom and Second Intermediate Period

addition to Franke's 'Personendaten'

Wolfram Grajetzki and Danijela Stefanović

GHP Egyptology 19

London 2012

GHP

This title is published by
Golden House Publications

London 2012

© Grajetzki, Stefanović

All rights reserved. No part of this publication may be reproduced or transmitted in any form or by any means, digital, electronic or mechanical, including photocopy, recording, or any information storage and retrieval system, without permission in writing from the author.

Golden House Publications
London

ISBN 978-1-906137-29-8

Printed in the UK
by CPI Group (UK) Ltd, Croydon, CR0 4YY

Contents

Introduction

The increasing body of knowledge on the Middle Kingdom and Second Intermediate Period is the result of studies of new data obtained through ongoing excavations, objects and documents whose existence has long been known, as well as others only published years after excavation or after their entering a museum collection. Due to the rapidly growing amount of data and number of publications, the various database models are not only useful tools for research – they are becoming a necessity.

Almost thirty years ago the late Detlef Franke published his work *Personendaten aus dem Mittleren Reich (20.-16. Jahrhundert V. Chr.): Dossiers 1-79,* Ägyptologische Abhandlungen 41, (Wiesbaden, 1984).[1] In this volume Franke collected 796 dossiers of people. These are data sets for men known from more than one source. His work remains an extremely useful research tool for dating objects and for revealing social networks in the Middle Kingdom. However, in the meantime, new material has been published (collections of various museums, rock inscriptions, provincial cemeteries). Therefore, the authors of this volume thought it was time for connecting the new data on officials with Franke's work in the form of additional dossiers. These new dossiers include the 12th up to the 17th Dynasty. As in Franke's volume, data of people from the 11th Dynasty has not been collected.

In this additional volume, first of all, the authors have tried to 'detect' new dossiers. In addition, the book also includes some of Franke's dossiers, e.g. those where it was possible to add new data (titles, family members, dating). In cases where this new material just repeats the existing information, the dossiers have not been included.[2] These include the dossiers of the 'vizier' *jmnjj*[3], the 'high stewards' (*jmj-r pr wr*) *ꜥ3b-nj*[4] and *tjtj*.[5] Other important examples are the datasets of the 'treasurers' (*jmj-r ḫtmt*) *snbj* (Franke's doss. 634) and *snb-sw-m-ꜥ(.j)* (Franke's doss.

[1] See review of R. Leprohon in *Chronique d'Egypte* 63, 1988, 264-267.

[2] Some examples: Doss. 591 (*sbk-ḥtp*), add: Vandekerckhove, Müller-Wollerman, *Die Felsinschriften des Wadi Hilâl*, O167 (pl. 165d-166a); cf. Franke, *JEA* 88, 2003, 263; Doss. 765 (*ddw-sbk / bbj*) statue fragment, Cambridge, FM E.SU.157 (unpublished).

[3] Franke, Doss. 116 (add Petrie, *Seasons*, pl. XVII, no. 594).

[4] Franke, Doss. 167 (add, London, UCL 80200, Petrie, *Weights and Measures*, pl. XXV, XXXVI, no. 3785A; Liverpool University Museum E.32, fragment of door frame from Abydos, Franke, *JEA* 87, 2001, 199).

[5] Franke, Doss. 732, (add Habachi, *Heqaib*, 77-78, nos. 50-51).

667).[6] For both these officials, new objects appeared after the publication of Franke's book, but none provide any substantially new data about them. However, 'new' stelae in particular provide important fresh information on administration, social networks and are useful for dating other important officials, such as the 'high steward' *jmnjj* (our Doss. 38), to give just one example. He is only more precisely datable after a stela was published mentioning him and *snb-sw-m-ʿ(.j)*.[7] Another important dossier not included in this volume are the monuments of the 'king's son' Nehesi (*z3-njswt nḥsj*). He is known from monuments and seals and was until recently dated to the beginning of the Second Intermediate Period.[8] A newly found stela dates him to the end of the period.[9] It might even indicate that there were two or more people with this name and title.[10]

The graphical pattern, the type and arrangement of data follow Franke's book. Unlike Franke's volume we have decided to include some dossiers of people known only from scarab seals, in case these seals are not just found in Martin, *Seals*[11] for making it easier to find these seals often published in different places. An exception are those seals where an official with different titles appears on different seals and from which it is possible to reconstruct a career.[12] An important omission is the scarab seals of the 'treasurer' (*jmj-r ḫtmt*) Har, known from more than 130 examples. He is the best attested official of all Egyptian history, but only from seals; he is not yet known from any other type of monument. His list of scarabs certainly deserves its own study and would be too large to include in a dossier.[13]

The numbering system used here starts again with number one. The numbers of Franke's volume are provided in the bibliography. This was done to keep an alphabetical order of the entries and at the same time not to have two numbering systems in the sequence of dossiers (that of Franke next to ours).

---

[6] Data collected in Grajetzki, *Two Treasurers*; for *snb-sw-m-ʿ(.j)* see also Grajetzki, in: *The Second Intermediate Period*, 307.

[7] Roccati, in: *Legacy of Berlev*, 111-114, pl. 7.

[8] Ryholt, *Second Intermediate Period*, 59, 376-378.

[9] Abd el-Maksoud, Valbelle, *RdE* 56 (2005), 8-11.

[10] Ben-Tor, *Scarabs, Chronology, and Interconnections*, 109-110; Ben-Tor, in: *The Second Intermediate Period*, 104-105.

[11] Martin, *Seals*.

[12] Examples include our Doss. (10), *jjj*; (184) *sbk-ʿ3 bbi*; (237), *ḏd-ptḥ ḏd.tw-snb*.

[13] List of scarabs, see: Ryholt, *Second Intermediate Period*, 60.

It should be noted that one dossier does not automatically mean that we are dealing with one person. Even in cases where a name and title are identical, there is always the possibility that these belong to two people with the same name and title who lived at about the same time. If the name, the title or both are rare, there is a higher chance of connecting the sources to one individual. However, even here, the dossier should be treated with some reservation if there are no additional data. Rare names might have been 'popular' for a very short time period, at a certain place or a certain time, giving the wrong impression that two attestations of a name, close in place and time, refer to the same person.

We are grateful to colleagues and institutions for their assistance in providing scientific data, sometimes not yet published. Photographs and information on sources were sent by Dr. Helmut Satzinger (Institut für Ägyptologie, Universität Wien), Dr. Emily Teeter (Oriental Institute of the University of Chicago), Dr. Guillemette Andreu (Musée du Louvre), Dr. Sara Caramello (Fondazione Museo delle Antichità Egizie di Torino) and Ashley Cooke (Liverpool, World Museum). We are also grateful to Paul Whelan for reading the English.

Datable dossiers:

Amenemhat I: 29, 31
Senusret I: 63, 111, 116, 170, 182, 208
Amenemhat II: 30, 95, 162, 170, 182, 208
Senusret II/Senusret III: 43, 58, 68, 82, 95, 117, 123, 160, 161, 235
Amenemhat III: 60, 93, 122, 127, 146, 157, 161, 204, 221, 233
Amenemhat IV: 236
Sobekhotep II – Neferhotep I: 9, 19, 38, 44, 64, 65, 89, 128, 154, 168, 176, 188, 194, 201, 210, 217, 229
Neferhotep I – Sebekhotep IV: 5, 18, 65, 71, 108, 126, 133, 198, 214
Sehkaenra Seankhptah: 101
Apophis Awoserre: 7

Abbreviations

ÄAT	Ägypten und Altes Testament
ANOC	Abydos North Offering Chapel (see Simpson, *ANOC*)
ASE	Archeological survey of Egypt
ASAE	Annales du Service des Antiquités de l'Égypte (SAE) (Cairo)
BAR	British Archaeological Reports International Series
BASOR	Bulletin of the American Schools of Oriental Research (South Hadley/New Haven)
BIFAO	Bulletin de l'Institut Français d'Archéologie Orientale (IFAO) (Cairo)
BiOr	Bibliotheca Orientalis (Leiden)
BMSAES	British Museum Studies in Ancient Egypt and Sudan
BSAE	British School of archaeology in Egypt
BSEG	Bulletin de la Société d'Égyptologie Genève (Geneva)
CAA	Corpus Antiquitatum Aegyptiacarum
CCG	Catalogue General du Musee du Caire (Cairo Museum)
CdÉ	Chronique d'Égypte; Bulletin périodique de la Fondation Égyptologique Reine Élisabeth, Bruxelles (Brussels)
Doss.	Dosssier,
EA	Egyptian Archaeology, the Bulletin of the Egypt Exploration Society (EES) (London)
EEF	Egypt Exploration Fund
ENIM	Égypte nilotique et méditerranéenne
FIFAO	Fouilles de l'Institut Français d'Archéologie Orientale du Caire
GM	Göttinger Miszellen (Göttingen)
HÄB	Hildesheimer ägyptologische Beiträge
IEJ	Israel Exploration Journal (Jerusalem)
JARCE	Journal of the American Research Center in Egypt (Boston/Princeton/New York/Cairo)
JEOL	Jaarbericht van het Vooraziatisch-egyptisch Genootschap Ex Oriente Lux (Leiden)
JEA	Journal of Egyptian Archaeology (EES, London)
MDAIK	Mitteilungen des Deutschen Archäologischen Instituts, Abteilung Kairo (DAIK) (Mainz/Cairo/Berlin/Wiesbaden)
MIFAO	Mémoires publiés par les membres de l'Institut français d'archéologie orientale du Caire
OLA	Orientalia Lovaniensia Analecta (Louvain)
OMRO	Oudheidkundige Mededelingen uit het Rijksmuseum van Oudheden (Leiden)
RdÉ	Revue d'Égyptologie (Paris)
RT	Recueil de traveaux relatifs à la philologie et à l'archéologie égyptiennes et assyriennes (Paris)

SAGA	Studien zur Archäologie und Geschichte Altägyptens
SAK	Studien zur Altägyptischen Kultur (Hamburg)
ZÄS	Zeitschrift für ägyptische Sprache und Altertumskunde (Berlin/Leipzig)

Bibliography

Abd el-Maksoud, Tell Heboua
M. Abd el-Maksoud, *Tell Heboua (1981-1991)*, Paris 1998
Abd el-Maksoud, Valbelle, *RdE* 56 (2005)
M. Abd el-Maksoud, D. Valbelle, 'Tell Heboua-Tjarou. L'apport de' l épigraphie', *RdE* 56 (2005), 1-44
Abd el-Raziq et al., *Ayn Soukhna*
M. Abd el-Raziq et al., *Les inscriptions d'Ayn Soukhna*, MIFAO 122, Cairo 2002.
Affara, *GM* 200, 2004
M. Affara, 'A Stela from Abydos in the Egyptian Museum, Cairo (Cg 20282)', *GM* 200, 2004, 13-26.
AIB I
Aegyptische Inschriften aus den Königlichen Museen zu Berlin I, Berlin 1913.
Allen, in: *Theban Necropolis*
J. P. Allen, 'The high officials of the early Middle Kingdom', in: N. Strudwick, J. H. Taylor (editors), *The Theban Necropolis, Past, Present and Future*, London 2003, 14-29
Allen, *BASOR* 352 (2008)
J. P. Allen , 'The Historical Inscription of Khnumhotep at Dahshur: Preliminary Report', *BASOR* 352, 2008, 29-39.
Allen, *Egyptian Stelae*
T. G. Allen, *Egyptian Stelae in Field Museum of Natural History*, Chicago 1936
Alliot, *Tell Edfou 1933*
M. Alliot, *Rapport sur les fouilles de Tell Edfou (1933)*, Cairo 1935.
Amer, *GM* 171, 1999, 19-23
A. A. M. A. Amer, 'A Stela from Liverpool', *GM* 171, 1999, 19-23
Andreau, *BSEG* 148, 2000
G. Andreau, 'La collection égyptienne du musée Dobreé à Nantes', *BSEG* 148, 2000, 18-30.
Arkell, JEA 36, 1950
J. Arkell, 'Varia Sudanica', *JEA* 36, 1950, 24-41.
Arnold, *Pyramid of Senwosret I*
D. Arnold, *The Pyramid of Senwosret I. The South Cemeteries of Lisht*, Vol. I, New York 1988.
Arnold, *Control Notes*
F. Arnold, *The Control Notes and Team Marks, The South Cemeteries of Lisht II,* New York 1990.
Arnold, *GM* 122, 1991
F. Arnold, 'The High Stewards of the Early Middle Kingdom', *GM* 122, 1991, 7-14.

Atallah, in: *Studies Radwan*
M. Atallah, Eine Stele aus dem Mittleren Reich im Ägyptischen Museum Kairo, in: *Studies in Honor of Ali Radwan*, ed. by K. Daoud, S. Bedier and S. Abd El-Fatah, Supplément ASAE: Cahier N° 34, Le Caire 2005, 151-158

Aufrère, *BIFAO* 85, 1985
S. Aufrère, 'A propos d'un bas de stèle du Musée des antiquités de Seine-Maritime (Rouen AEg. 348 = Inv. 1857.4)', *BIFAO* 85, 1985, 33-40.

Awad, *SAK* 39, 2010
K. H. Awad, Zwei Totengedenksteine des späten Mittleren Reiches im Louvre, *SAK* 39, 2010, 19-38, pl. 1-3.

Ballerini, *Bessarione* 7, 1910
Fr. Ballerini, 'Antichità egiziane nel Museo Civico di Como', *Bessarione* 7, 1910, 210-237.

Baligh, *JARCE* 44, 2008
R. Baligh, 'Three Middle Kingdom Stelae from the Egyptian Museum in Cairo', *JARCE* 44, 2008, 169-184.

Barbotin, *Musée Granet*
C. Barbotin, *Musée Granet, Aix*-en-*Provence*: *Collection égyptienne*, Aix-en-Provence 1995.

Bard-Fattovich, *Harbor*
K. A. Bard – R. Fattovich, *Harbor of the Pharaohs to the Land of Punt. Archaeological Investigations at Mersa/Wadi Gawasis Egypt 2001-2005*, Napoli 2007.

Ben-Tor, *BASOR* 294, 1994
D. Ben-Tor, 'The Historical Implications of Middle Kingdom Scarabs Found in Palestine Bearing Private Names and Titles of Officials', *BASOR* 294, 1994, 7-22.

Ben-Tor, *IMJ* 8, 1988
D. Ben-Tor, 'Scarabs Bearing Titles and Private Names of Officials from the Middle Kingdom and the Second Intermediate Period (c. 2050-1550 B.C.E.)', *IMJ* 8, 1988, 35-46.

Ben-Tor, *Scarab*
D. Ben-Tor, *The Scarab: A Reflection of Ancient Egypt*, Jerusalem 1993.

Ben-Tor, *Scarabs, Chronology, and Interconnections*
D. Ben-Tor, Scarabs, *Chronology, and Interconnections, Egypt and Palestine in the Second Intermediate Period*, OBO, Series Archaeologica 27, Fribourg, Göttingen 2007

Ben-Tor, in: *The Second Intermediate Period*
D. Ben-Tor, 'Sequence and Chronologiy of Second Intermediate Period Royal-Name Scarabs, based on excavated Series from Egypt and the Levant', in: *The Second Intermediate Period (Thirteenth-Seventeenth Dynasties): Current Research, Future Prospects*, ed. by M. Mareé, OLA 192, Louven 2010, 91-108

Berlev-Hodjash, *Sculpture of Ancient Egypt*
O.D. Berlev – S. Hodjash, *Sculpture of Ancient Egypt in the Collection of the Pushkin State Museum of Fine Arts: Catalogue*, Moscow 2004.

Bi'r Minayh
Bi'r Minayh: Report on the Survey 1998-2004, ed. by U. Luft, Budapest 2010.

Birch, *Catalogue*
S. Birch, *Catalogue of the Collection of Egyptian Antiquities at Alnwick Castle*, London 1890.

Blackman, *Meir III*
A. M. Blackman, *The Rock Tombs of Meir III*, ASE 24, London 1915.

Boeser, *Leiden*
P.A.A. Boeser, *Beschrijving van de Egyptische verzameling in het Rijksmuseum van Oudheden te Leiden. De monumenten van den tijd tusschen het Oude en het Middelrijk en van het Middelrijk. Eerste afdeeling: Stèles*, Gravenhage 1909.

Bolshakov-Quirke, *Hermitage*
A. O. Bolshakov – S. Quirke, *The Middle Kingdom Stelae in the Hermitage*, Utrecht-Paris 1999.

Borchardt, *ZÄS* 37, 1899
L. Borchardt, ‚Der zweite Papyrufund von Kahun und die zeitliche Festlegung des mittleren Reiches der ägyptischen Geschichte', *ZÄS* 37, 1899, 89-103.

Borchardt, *Statuen und Statuetten*
L. Borchardt, *Statuen und Statuetten von Königen und Privatleuten im Museum von Kairo, Nr. 1-1294, Teil 2: Text und Tafeln zu Nr. 381-653*, Berlin 1925.

Bosticco, *Stele*
S. Bosticco, *Le Stele Egiziane dall'Antico al Nuovo Regno*, Roma 1959.

Bosticco, Rosati, *Aegyptus* 83, 2003
S. Bosticco, G. Rosati, 'Il sarcophago di Amenemhet-seneb a Firenze', *Aegyptus* 83, 2003, 15-52.

van Bothmer, *Ancient Art from New York Private Collections*
D. van Bothmer, *Ancient Art from New York Private Collections Catalogue of an Exhibition held at The Metropolitan Museum of Art,*New York 1961.

Bourriau, *Pharaohs and Mortals*
J. Bourriau, *Pharaohs and Mortals. Egyptian Art in the Middle Kingdom,* Cambridge 1988.

Capart, *Monuments égyptiens*
J. Capart, *Recueil de monuments égyptiens*, Brussels 1902.

Carnarvon - Carter, *Five Years' Exploration at Thebes*
G. E. S. Carnarvon – H. Carter, *Five Years' Exploration at Thebes. A Record of Work Done 1907-1911*, London 1912.

Clèdat, *BIFAO* 1, 1901
M. J. Clèdat, 'Notes archeologiques et philologiques', *BIFAO* 1, 1901, 87-99.

Clèdat, *BIFAO* 2, 1902
M. J. Clèdat, 'Notes archeologiques et philologiques', *BIFAO* 2, 1902, 41-70.

Clère, *JEA* 68, 1982
J.J. Clère, 'La stele de Sânkhptah, chambellan du roi Râhotep', *JEA* 68, 1982, 60-68.
Collier - Quirke, *Accounts*
M. Collier - S. Quirke, *The UCL Lahun Papyri: Accounts,* BAR 1471, Oxford 2006.
Collier - Quirke, *Letters*
M. Collier - S. Quirke, *The UCL Lahun Papyri: Letters,* BAR 1083, Oxford 2002.
Cooney -Tyrrell, *PalArch's Journal of Archaeology of Egypt/Egyptology* 4,1.2, 2005
K. M. Cooney – J. Tyrrell, 'Scarabs in the Los Angeles County Museum of Art', *PalArch's Journal of Archaeology of Egypt/Egyptology* 4,1.2, 2005, 15-98.
Černy, *IS*
A. Gardiner - T.E. Peet – J. Černy, *The Inscriptions of Sinai*, vol. I – vol. II: Introductions and Plates, London 1952-1955.
Darnell, *Theban Desert Road Survey* I
J.C. Darnell, et al., *Theban Desert Road Survey in the Egyptian Western Desert I: The Rock Inscriptions of Gebel Tjauti in the Theban Western Desert, Part 1, and the Rock Inscriptions of the Wadi el Hôl,* Chicago 2002.
Darnell, *JARCE* XXXVI, 1999
R. F. Friedman, with contributions by A. Maish, A. G. FAhmy, J. C. Darnell, E. D. Johnson, Preliminary Report on Field Work at Hierkonpolis 1996-1998, *JARCE* XXXVI 1999, 1-35
Darnell, Darnell, *Nekhen News*, Fall 1996 (8)
John Darnell, Deborah Darnell, 'Pharaonic Rock Inscriptions at Gebel Norée', *Nekhen News*, Fall 1996 (8), 6-7.
David, *Two Brothers*
R. David, *The Two Brothers, Death and the Afterlife in Middle Kingdom Egypt*, Bolton 2007
Delange, *Catalogue des statues égyptiennes*
E. Delange, *Catalogue des statues égyptiennes du Moyen Empire, 2060-1560 avant J.C.*, Paris 1987.
DeM
J. de Morgan et al, *Catalogue des monuments et inscriptions de l'Egypte antique I: De la frontière de Nubie à Kom Ombos*, Vienna 1894.
Donohue, in: *Studies Malek*
V. A. Donohue, A Latopolitan Family of the Late Middle Kingdom, in: *Sitting Beside Lepsius. Studies in Honour of Jaromir Malek at the Griffith Institute*, ed. by D. Magee et al, Leuven 2009, 115-127.
Dreyer at al., *MDAIK* 64, 2008
G. Dreyer at al., 'Stadt und Tempel von Elephantine 33./34./35. Grabungsbericht', *MDAIK* 64, 2008, 63-151.

Dunham, *Second Cataract Forts* II
D. Dunham, *Uronarti Shalfak Mirgissa. Second Cataract Forts* II, Boston 1967.
Engelbach, *ASAE* 22, 1922
R. Engelbach, 'Steles and Tables of Offerings of the Late Middle Kingdom from Tell Edfu', *ASAE* 22, 1922, 113-123.
Engelbach, *Harageh*
R. Engelbach, *Harageh*, BSAE 28, London 1923
Engelbach - Townsend, *ASAE* 33, 1933
R. Engelbach - T. C. Townsend, 'A XIIth Dynasty Inscriptions near the Cairo-Suez Road', *ASAE* 33, 1933, 1-5.
Fakhry, *Monuments of Sneferu* II[2]
A. Fakhry, *The Monuments of Sneferu at Dahshur, Vol. II[2], The Valley Temple. Part* II*: The Finds, Cairo 1961.*
Firth, Gunn, *Teti Pyramid Cemeteries, I*
C. M. Firth, B. Gunn, *Teti Pyramid Cemeteries, Vol. I*, Cairo 1920
Fischer, *Egyptian Titles*
H. G. Fischer, *Egyptian Titles of the Middle Kingdom. A Supplement to Wm.Ward's Index, Parts I-III. Corrections and Comments*, New York 1997.[2]
Fischer, *Egyptian Studies* III
H. G. Fischer, *Egyptian Studies III. Varia Nova*, New York 1996.
Fischer, *RdE* 24, 1972
H. G. Fischer, '*sḫꜣ.sn* (Florence 1774)', *RdE* 24, 1972, 64-71.
Fischer-Elfert - Grimm, *ZÄS* 130, 2003
H. W. Fischer-Elfret - A. Grimm, 'Autobiographie und Apotheose', *ZÄS* 130, 2003, 60-80.
Franke, in: *Middle Kingdom Studies*
D. Franke, 'The Career of Khnumhotep III of Beni Hasan and the so-called "Decline of the Nomarchs"', in: *Middle Kingdom Studies*, ed. by S. Quirke, New Malden 1991, 51-67.
Franke, *Doss.*
D. Franke, *Personendaten aus dem Mittleren Reich (20.-16. Jahrhundert v. Chr.). Dossiers 1-796*, Wiesbaden 1984.
Franke, *JEA* 71, 1985, 175-176
D. Franke, 'An important family from Abydos of the Seventeenth Dynasty', *JEA* 71, 1985, 175-176.
Franke, *MDAIK* 57, 2001
D. Franke, ‚Drei neue Stelen des Mittleren Reiches von Elephantine', *MDAIK* 57, 2001, 15-34.
Franke, *OMRO* 68, 1988
D. Franke, ‚Die Hockerstatue des Sonbso-Mei in Leiden und Statuen mit nach oben gerichteten Handflächen,' *OMRO* 68, 1988, 59-76.
Franke, *SAK* 10, 1983
D. Franke, 'Stele Inv.Nr. 4403 im Landesmuseum in Oldenburg - zur Lebensmittelproduktion in der 13. Dynastie' *SAK* 10, 1983, 157-178.

Franke, *Heqaib*
D. Franke, *Das Heiligtum des Heqaibauf Elephantine*, SAGA 9, Heidelberg 1994.
Franke, *JEA* 87, 2001
D. Franke, review of Grajetzki, *Beamte*, *JEA*, 87, 2001, 197-200.
Franke, *JEA* 88, 2002
D. Franke, review of Vandekerckhove, Müller-Wollerman, *Die Felsinschriften des Wadi Hilâl, JEA* 88, 2002, S. 261 – 263.
Franke, in: *Studies Assmann*,
D. Franke, 'Middle Kingdom Hymns and other sundry religious texts - an inventory', in: *Egypt - temple of the whole world; studies in honour of Jan Assmann*, ed. by S. Meyer, Leiden 2003, 95-135.
Franke, in: *Die Pyramidenanlage des Königs Nub-Cheper-Re Intef*
D. Franke, 'Die Stele des Jayseneb aus der Schachtanlage K01.12', *Die Pyramidenanlage des Königs Nub-Cheper-Re Intef in Dra' Abu el-Naga: ein Vorbericht*, Hrsg. D. Polz – A. Seiler, Mainz 2003
Freed, in: *Studies Simpson*
R. Freed, 'Stela Workshops of Early Dynasty 12', in: *Studies in Honor of William Kelly Simpson*, ed. by P. Der Manuelian, Vol. I, Boston 1996, 297-336.
Gabra - Nagib, *Varia Aegyptiaca* 10 (2-3), 1995
G. Gabra - R, Nagib, 'Zu einem Opferständer eines Hohenpriesters von Heliopolis des Mittleren Reiches', *Varia Aegyptiaca*, 10 (2-3), 1995, 101-104.
Gamer-Wallert – Gerishammer, *Ägyptische Kunst*
A. Gamer-Wallert – R. Gerishammer, *Ägyptische Kunst*, Karlsruhe 1992
Garstang, *El-Arabah*
J. Garstang, *El Arabah: A Cemetery of the Middle Kingdom*, BSAE 6, London 1901
Garstang, *Burial customs*
J. Garstang, *The Burial Customs of Ancient Egypt as illustrated by the Tombs of the Middle Kingdom*, London 1907
Gasse-Randot, *Séhel*
A. Gasse – V. Randot, *Les inscriptions de Séhel*, MIFAO 26, Le Caire 2007.
Gatty, *Mayer Collection*
C. T. Gatty, *Catalogue of the Mayer Collection. Part I: The Egyptian Antiquities*, Liverpool 1879.
Gayet, *Stèles de la XIIe dynastie*
E. Gayet, *Musée du Louvre. Stèles de la XIIe dynastie*, Paris 1886.
Giveon, *CdE* 98, 1974
R. Giveon, 'Hyksos Scarabs with Names of Kings and Officials from Canaan', *CdE* 98, 1974, 222-233.
Giveon, *GM* 67, 1983
R. Giveon, 'A Second Look at Some Inscribed Scarabs', *GM* 67, 1983, 33-37.

Giveon, *IEJ* 34, 1984
R. Giveon, 'A Middle Kindgom Statue from Serabit el-Khadim in Sinai', *IEJ* 34, 1984, 154-155.
Götter, Menschen, Pharaonen
Götter Menschen Pharaonen. 3500 Jahre ägyptische Kultur, *Meisterwerke aus der Ägyptisch-Orientalischen Sammlung des Kunsthistorischen Museums Wien*, ed. by W. Seipel, Berlin 1996.
Grajetzki, *GM* 156 (1997)
W. Grajetzki, 'Bemerkungen zu den Bürgermeistern (HAtj-a) von Qaw el-Kebir im Mittleren Reich', *GM* 156 (1997), 55-62
Grajetzki, *Beamte*
W. Grajetzki, *Die höchsten Beamten der ägyptischen Zentralverwaltung zur Zeit des Mittleren Reiches*, Achet A2, Berlin 2000.
Grajetzki, *Two Treasurers*
W. Grajetzki, *Two Treasurers of the Late Middle Kingdom*, BAR 1007, London 2001
Grajetzki,, *SAK* 23, 2006
W. Grajetzki, 'Another early source for the Book of the Dead: The Second Intermediate Period Burial D 25 at Abydos', *SAK* 23, 2006, 205-216
Grajetzki, *Court Officials*
W. Grajetzki, *Court Officials of the Egyptian Middle Kingdom*, London 2009
Grajetzki, *RdE* 60, 2009
W. Grajetzki, Women and writing, Stela Louvre C187, *RdE* 60, 2009, 209-14
Grajetzki, *GM* 224, 2010
W. Grajetzki, 'Remarks on women with male names: Stela Glasgow 1923.33.ac in the Kelvingrove Art Gallery and Museum', *GM* 224, 2010, 47-58.
Grajetzki, in: *The Second Intermediate Period*
W. Grajetzki, 'Notes on the Administration in the Second Intermediate Period', in: *The Second Intermediate Period (Thirteenth-Seventeenth Dynasties): Current Research, Future Prospects*, ed. by M. Mareé, OLA 192, Louven 2010, 305-312.
Grajetzki, *Zemathor*
W. Grajetzki, *The coffin of Zemathor and other rectangular coffins of the late Middle Kingdom and Second Intermediate Period*, GHP Egyptology 15, London 2010
Gratien, in: *Mélanges Vercoutter*
B. Gratien, 'La nécropole SAC 4 de l'île de Sai: L'occupation Kerma', in: *Mélanges offerts à Jean Vercoutter*, eds. F Geus – F. Thill, Paris 1985, 93-100.
Gratien, in: *Nubische Studien*
B. Gratien, 'Premieres constatations sur les empreintes de sceaux de la fortresse de Mirgissa', in: M. Krause (editor) *Nubische Studien*, Mainz 1989.

Gratien, *Prosopographie*
B. Gratien, *Prosopographie des Nubiens et des Égyptiens en Nubie avant le Nouvel Empire Cahier de recherches de l'Institut de papyrologie et d'égyptologie de Lille. Supplément* 3, Lille 1991.
Griffith, Newberry, *El Bersheh II*
F. Ll. Griffith, P. E.; Newberry, Percy E., *El Bersheh II*, London 1895.
Grimm, *Zeitschrift für Wissenschaft und Kunst in Bayern* 3, 2002
A. Grimm, 'Herrn Lotosblumes Wiedervereinigung', *Zeitschrift für Wissenschaft und Kunst in Bayern* 3, 2002, 42-46.
Guichard, *RdE* 58, 2007
S. Guichard, 'Une collection d'antiquités égyptiennes méconnue. La collection Thédenat-Duvent', *RdE* 58, 2007, 201-228.
Habachi, *Heqaib*,
L. Habachi, *Elephantine IV: The Sanctuary of Heqaib*, (Elephantine IV), Archäologische Veröffernţlichungen 33, Mainz am Rhein 1985.
Habachi, *Tavole d'offerta are e bacilli da libagione*
L. Habachi, *Tavole d'offerta are e bacilli da libagione, n. 22001-22067*, Catalogo del Museo Egizio di Torino II, Torino 1977
Hayes, *Papyrus of the Late Middle Kingdom*
W.C. Hayes, *A Papyrus of the Late Middle Kingdom in the Brooklyn Museum*, Brooklyn 1955.
Hayes, *Scepter of Egypt*
W.C. Hayes, The *Scepter of Egypt: A Background for the Study of the Egyptian Antiquities in The Metropolitan Museum of Art* I-II, New York 1955-1959.
Hamza, *MDAIK* 63, 2007
K. A. Hamza, 'Zwei Stelen aus dem Mittleren Reich im Louvre', *MDAIK* 63, 2007, 53-67.
Hein – Satzinger, *Stelen des Mittleren Reiches*
I. Hein – H. Satzinger, *Stelen des Mittleren Reiches I, einschließlich der I. und II Zwischenzeit,* CAA, Kunshistorisches Museum Wien 4, Mainz 1989.
I. Hein – H. Satzinger, *Stelen des Mittleren Reiches II, einschließlich der I. und II Zwischenzeit,* CAA, Kunshistorisches Museum Wien 7, Mainz 1993.
Hintze-Reineke, *FSN*
F. Hintze - W. F. Reineke, *Felsinschriften aus dem sudanesischen Nubien,* Teil I + II, Band I, Berlin 1989.
HTBM
Scott-Moncrieff, P.D., *Hieroglyphic Texts from Egyptian Stelae etc. in the British Museum* II, London 1912.
Hall, H.R., Lambert, E.J., *Hieroglyphic Texts from Egyptian Stelae etc. in the British Museum* III, London 1912.
Hall, H.R., Lambert, E.J., *Hieroglyphic Texts from Egyptian Stelae etc. in the British Museum* IV, London 1913.

Horváth, *Life and Afterlife*

Z. Horváth, 'Remarks on the Temple of Heqet and a Sarcastic Letter from El-Lahun', in: S. Grallert, W. Grajetzki (eds.) *Life and Afterlife in the Middle Kingdom and Second Intermediate Period*, GHP Egyptology 7, London 2007, 81-90

El-Husseiny - Khafagy, *EA* 36, 2010, 21-24

S. el-Husseiny - A. O. Khafagy, 'The Dahshur tomb of the vizier Siese rediscovered', *EA* 36, 2010, 21-24.

James, *Inscriptions*

T. G. H. James, *Corpus of Hieroglyphic Inscriptions in the Brooklyn Museum I, From Dynasty I to the End of Dynasty XVIII*, Brooklyn 1974

Jaroš-Deckert, *Statuen*

B. Jaroš-Deckert, *Statuen des Mittleren Reiches und der 18. Dynastie, CAA, Kunsthistorisches Museum Wien, Lieferung 1*, Mainz 1987.

Kaiser, *Berlin*

W. Kaiser, *Ägyptisches Museum Berlin*, Berlin 1967.

Kamal, *ASAE*, 3 (1902)

A. B. Kamal, 'Fouilles à Deir el-Barchè executes dans les six premiers mois de de l'année par M. Antonio de Mallawi', *ASAE* 3 (1902), 276-282

Kamal, *ASAE* 11, 1911

A. B. Kamal, 'Rapport sur les fouilles exécutées dans la zone comprise entre Deirout an Nord et Déir-el-Ganadlah, an sud', *ASAE* 11, 1911, 3-39.

Kamal, *ASAE* 12, 1912

A. B. Kamal, 'Rapport sur les fouilles exécutées dans la zone comprise entre Deirout an Nord et Déir-el-Ganadlah, an sud', *ASAE* 11, 1911, 97-127.

Kamal, *ASAE* 14, 1914

A. B. Kamal, 'Rapport sur les fouilles exécutées dans la zone comprise entre Deirout an Nord et Déir-el-Hanadlah, an sud', *ASAE* 14, 1914, 45-87.

Kamal, *ASAE* 16, 1916

A. B. Kamal, 'Fouilles à Deir Dronka et à Assiout (1913-1914)', *ASAE* 16, 1916, 65-114.

Kamal, *Tables d'offrandes*

A. B. Kamal, *Tables d'offrandes* I-II, Le Caire, CGC, 1906-1909.

Kitchen, *Catalogue*

K. A. Kitchen, *Catalogue of the Egyptian Collection in the National Museum, Rio de Janeiro*, Warminster 1990.

Koefoed-Petersen, *Stele eg. Kopenhague*

O. Koefoed-Petersen, *Les Stèles égyptiennes. Publications de la Gliptothèque Ny Carlsberg,* Copenhague 1948.

Krauspe, *Statuen und Statuetten*

R. Krauspe, *Katalog Agyptischer Sammiungen in Leipzig. Band 1. Statuen und Statuetten*, Mainz 1997.

Krauss, Orientalia 62 (1993)

R. Krauss, 'Zur Problematik der Nubienpolitik Kamoses sowie der Hyksosherrschaft in Oberägypten', *Orientalia* 62, 1993, 17-29

Lange-Schäfer, *CCG*
H. O. Lange - H. Schäfer, *Grab- und Denksteine des Mittleren Reiches im Museum von Kairo. No. 20001-20780*. I-II, CGC, Berlin 1902-1908.
Leahy, *GM* 44, 1981
A. Leahy, 'A Stela of the Second Intermediate Period', *GM* 44, 1981, 23-28.
Lembke, *GM* 150, 1996
K. Lembke, 'Unter falschem Namen: Der sog. Chertihotep (Berlin ÄM 15700)', *GM* 150, 1996, 81-86.
Leospo in: *Passato e futuro del Museo Egizio di Torino (Archivi di Archeologia)*
E. Leospo, 'Coperchio del sarcofago di Nakhti, testa do sarcofago antropoide, cassetta per canopi di Uahkha', in: *Passato e futuro del Museo Egizio di Torino (Archivi di Archeologia)*, ed. by A-M. Donadoni-Roveri Toroni 1988,
Leprohon, in: *Studies Simpson*
R. J. Leprohon, 'A Late Middle Kingdom Stela in a Private Collection', in: *Studies in Honor of William Kelly Simpson*, Boston 1996, 523-531
Lichtheim, *Autobiographies*
M. Lichtheim, *Ancient Egyptian autobiographies chiefly of the Middle Kingdom: A study and an anthology*, Freiburg 1988
Luft, *Briefe aus Ilahun*,
U. Luft, *Urkunden zur Chronologie der späten 12. Dynastie: Briefe aus Ilahun*, Vienna 2006.
Lüscher, *Kanopenkästen*
B. Lüscher, *Untersuchungen zu den ägyptischen Kanopenkästen – Vom Alten Reich bis zum Ende der Zweiten Zwischenzeit*, HÄB 31, Hildesheim 1990
Mahfouz, *Afrique & Orient* 41, 2006
El-Sayed Mahfouz, 'Les ostraca hiératiques du Ouadi Gaouasis', *Afrique & Orient* 41, 2006, 31-34.
Marée, *Afrique & Orient* 53, 2009
M. Marée, 'Nouvelles données sur l'élite d'Edfou à la fin de la XVIIe dynastie',
Afrique & Orient 53, 2009, 11-24.
Marée, *BiOr* 66, 2009
M. Marée, 'The 12th –17th Dynasties at Gebel el-Zeit: A Closer Look at the Inscribed Royal Material', *BiOr* 66, 2009, 148-162.
Marée, *BMSAES* 12, 2009
M. Marée, 'Edfu under the Twelfth to Seventeenth Dynasties: The monuments in the National Museum of Warsaw', *BMSAES* 12, 2009, 31-92.
Mareé, in: *The Second Intermediate Period*
M. Mareé, 'A sculpture workshop at Abydos from the late Sixteenth or early Seventeenth Dynasty', in: *The Second Intermediate Period (Thirteenth-Seventeenth Dynasties): Current Research, Future Prospects*, ed. by M. Mareé, OLA 192, Louven 2010, 241-281.
Meeks, *ENIM* 2, 2009
D. Meeks, 'Une stèle de donation de la Deuxième Période intermédiaire', *ENIM* 2, 2009, 129-154

Melandri, *Vicino & Medio Oriente* XV (2011)
I. Melandri, 'Nuove considerazioni su una statua da Qaw el-Kebir al museo delle antichità egizie di Torino', *Vicino & Medio Oriente* XV (2011), 249-270
Martin, *MDAIK* 35, 1979
G. T. Martin, 'Private Name Seals in the Alnwick Castle Collection', MDAIK 35, 1979, 215-226.
Maspero, *RT* 13, 1890
G. Maspero, 'Monuments égyptiens du Musée de Marseille', *RT* 13, 1890, 113-126.
Martin, *Seals*
G. T. Martin, *Egyptian Administrative and Private-Name Seals*, Oxford 1971
Martin, *Stelae*
G. T. Martin, *Stelae from Egypt and Nubia in the Fitzwilliam Museum Cambridge, c. 3000 BC- AD 1150*, Cambridge 2005.
de Meulenaere, *CdE* 60, 1985
H. de Meulenaere, 'Les monuments d'un haut dignitaire de la 13e dynastie', *CdE* 60, 1985, 75-84
Miniaci, in: *Il tempio e il suo personale nell'antico Egitto*
G. Miniaci, 'Il potere nella 17a dinastia: il titolo "figlio del re" e il ripensamento delle strutture amministrative nel Secondo Periodo Intermedio', in: *Il tempio e il suo personale nell'antico Egitto. Atti del quarto Colloquio, Bologna - 24/25 settembre 2008 a cura di Sergio Pernigotti e Marco Zecchi*, Imola (BO) 2010, 99-131.
Miniaci, *Rishi Coffins*
G. Miniaci, *The Rishi Coffins and the Funerary Culture of Second Intermediate Period Egypt*, GHP Egyptoloy 17, London 2011
Jørgensen, *Catalogue Egypt I (3000-1550 B.C.)*
M. Jørgensen, *Catalogue Egypt I (3000-1550 B.C.), Ny Carlsberg Glyptotek*, Copenhagen 1996
Monnet Saleh, *Les antiquités égyptiennes de Zagreb*
J. Monnet Saleh, *Les antiquités égyptiennes de Zagreb*, Paris 1970.
Moret, *Stèles*
A. Moret, *Catalogue du Musée Guimet. Galerie égyptienne, stèles, bas-reliefs, monuments divers*, Paris 1909.
de Morgan, *Dahchour 1894-1895*
J. de Morgan, *Dahchour 1894-1895*, Vienna 1903
Muscarella, *Ancient Art*
O. W. Muscarella, *Ancient Art. The Norbert Schimmel Collection*, Mainz 1974.
Collezione Egiziana di Napoli
Soperintendenza Archaeologica per province di Napoli e Caserta (editor): *La Collezione Egiziana del Museo Archeologica Nazionale di Napoli*, Napoli 1989
Newberry, *Beni Hasan*
P. E. Newberry, *Beni Hasan* I-II, ASE 1-2, London 1893-1894.

Newberry, *El Berscheh I*
P. E. Newberry, *El Berscheh I*, ASE 3, London 1895.
Newberry, *Funerary Statuettes*
P. E. Newberry, *Funerary Statuettes and Model Sarcophagi* I-III, CGC, Cairo 1930-1957.
Page, *Egyptian Sculpture*
A. Page, *Egyptian sculpture: Archaic to Saite from the Petrie Collection*, Warminster 1976.
Niccacci, *Scarabs*
A. Niccacci, *Hyksos Scarabs*, Jerusalem 1980.
Patch, *Reflections of Greatness*
D. C. Patch, *Reflections of Greatness: Ancient Egypt at The Carnegie Museum of Natural History*, Pittsburgh 1990.
Pernigotti, *Antichità egiziane del Museo Gaetano Chierici*
S. Pernigotti, *Antichità egiziane del Museo Gaetano Chierici di paletnologia Cataloghi dei Civici musei Comune di Reggio Emilia*, Reggio Emilia 1991.
Petrie, *Gizeh and Rifeh*
W. M. F. Petrie, *Gizeh and Rifeh*, BSAE 13, London 1907.
Petrie, *Season*
W. M. F. Petrie, *A season in Egypt 1887*, London 1888.
Petrie, *Weights and Measures*
W. M. F. Petrie, *Ancient Weights and Measures*, BSAE 39, London 1926
Petrie - Weigall, *Abydos* I
W. M. F. Petrie – A. E. P. Weigall, *Abydos* I, EEF 22, London 1902.
Petrie - Griffith, *Abydos* II
W. M. F. Petrie – F. Ll. Griffith, *Abydos* II, EEF 24, London 1903.
Pierret, *Inscr. du Louvre* II
P. Pierret, *Recueil d'Inscriptions inédites du Musée égyptien du Louvre* II, Paris 1878.
von Pilgrim, *Untersuchungen*
C, von Pilgrim, Elephantine XVIII, *Untersuchungenin der Stdat des Mittleren Reiches und der Zweiten Zwischenzeit*, (Elephantine XVIII), AV 91, Mainz am Rhein 1996.
Pirelli, *RdÉ* 58, 2007
R. Pirelli, 'Two New Stelae from Mersa Gawasis', *RdÉ* 58, 2007, 87-106.
Polz,, in *Für die Ewigkeit geschaffen*
D. Polz, 'Die Ausgrabungen des Deutschen Archäologischen Instituts in Dra' Abu el-Naga', in Polz (editor),, in Für die Ewigkeit geschaffen, Die Särge des Imeni un der Geheset, Mainz am Rhein 2007, 14-24.
Quirke, in: *Excavating Egypt*
S. Quirke, 'Weight inscribed for the treasurer Herfu', in: *Excavating Egypt*, Atlanta 2005, 116, no. 86.
Quirke, *JEOL* 37, 2003
S. Quirke, 'Two thirteenth dynasty heart scarabs', *JEOL* 37, 2003, 31-40.

Quirke, *RdÉ* 39, 1988
S. Quirke, 'State and Labour in the Middle Kingdom: A Reconsideration of the Term xnrt', *RdE* 39, 1988, 83-106.
Quirke, *RdÉ* 51, 2000
S. Quirke, 'Six hieroglyphic inscriptions in University College Dublin', *RdÉ* 51, 2000, 223-251.
Ralston, in: *Legacy of Berlev*, 107-110
I. Ralston, 'The Stela of Ibi son of Iiqi in the Marischal Museum, University of Aberdeen', in: *Discovering Egypt from the Neva. The Egyptological Legacy of Oleg D. Berlev*, ed. by S. Quirke, Berlin 2003, 107-110
Ramond, *Musée Labit*
P. Ramond, *Les stèles égyptiennes du Musée G. Labit à Toulouse*, Cairo 1977.
Regen – Soukiassian, *Gebel El-Zeit* II
I. Regen – G. Soukiassian, *Gebel El-Zeit* II *Le matériel inscrit. Moyen Empire - Nouvel Empire*, FIFAO 57, Le Caire 2008.
Rigault, Delange, *RdE* 60 (2009)
P. Rigault, É. Delange, 'Le lit funéraire de Djehoutihotep (Louvre AF 9170)', *RdÉ* 60 (2009), 63-138
Rio de Janeiro, see: Kitchen, *Catalogue*
Roccati, in: *Legacy of Berlev*
A. Roccati, 'Quattro Stele del Medio Regno', in: *Discovering Egypt from the Neva. The Egyptological Legacy of Oleg D. Berlev*, ed. by S. Quirke, Berlin 2003, 111-121.
Rummel, in: *Begegnung*
U. Rummel, 'Dra' Abu el-Naga', in U. Rummel (editor), *Begegnung mit der Vergangenheit, 100 Jahre in Ägypten*, Cairo 2007, 29-53.
Russo, *Territory w*
B. Russo, *The territory w and related titles during the Middle Kingdom and the Second Intermediate Period*, GHP Egyptoloy 13, London 2010.
Ryhold, *Second Intermediate Period*
K. Ryhold, *The Political Situatiion in Egypt during the Second Intermediate Period,* Carsten Niebuhr Institute Publications 20, Copenhagen 1997
Sadek, *Wadi el-Hudi*
A. I. Sadek, *The Amethyst mining inscriptions of Wadi el-Hudi* I-II, Warminster 1980-1985.
Satzinger-Stefanović, in: *From Illahun to Djeme*
H. Satzinger – D. Stefanović, 'The domestic servant of the palace rn-snb', in: *Papers Presented in Honour of Ulrich Luft*, ed. by E. Bechtold, A. Gulyás, and A. Hasznos, London 2011, 241-245.
Sauneron, *BIFAO* 51 (1952)
S. Sauneron, 'Le « Chancelier du Dieu » [*ḫtmw-nṯr*] dans son double rôle d'embaumeur et de prêtre d'Abydos', *BIFAO* 51 (1952), 137-171
Scharff, *ZÄS* 57, 1922
A. Scharff, 'Ein Rechnungsbuch des königlichen Höfes aus der 13. Dynastie (Papyrus Boulaq Nr. 18)', *ZÄS* 57, 1922, 51-68; 1**-24**.

Schildkraut - Solia, *Egypt at the Merrin Gallery*
L. Schildkraut – V. L. Solia, *Egypt at the Merrin Gallery*, New York 1992.
Schmitz, *Königssohn*
B. Schmitz *Untersuchungen zum Titel s3-njswt "Königssohn"*, Bonn 1976.
Sharpe, *Egyptian Inscriptions* II
S. Sharpe, *Egyptian Inscriptions from the British Museum and other Sources* II, London 1855.
van Siclen, III, Schoske (editor), *Akten des vierten Internationalen Aegyptologischen Kongresse*
C. C. van Siclen, III, 'The Mayors of Basta in th Middle Kingdom', in: S. Schoske (editor), *Akten des vierten Internationalen Aegyptologischen Kongresses, Muenchen 1985* (Studien zur Altaegyptischen Kultur, Beihefte 4), Hamburg 1991, 187-194
Simpson, *ANOC*
W. K. Simpson, *The Terrace of the Great God at Abydos: The Offering Chapels of Dynasties 12 and 13*, New Haven-Philadelphia 1974.
Simpson, in: *Pyramid Studies*, 57-60, pls. 14-15
W. K. Simpson, Lepsius Pyramid IV at Dahshur: the Mastaba of Si-Ese, Vizier of Amenemhat II, in: *Pyramid Studies and other Eassys presented to I.E.S. Edwards*, ed. by J. Baines, T.G. H. James, A. Leahy, A.F. Shire, London 1988, 57-60, pls. 14-15
Simpson, *Inscribed Materials*
W. K. Simpson, *Inscribed Material from the Pennsylvania-Yale Excavations at Abydos*, New Haven - Philadelphia 1995.
Small Sculpture from Ancient Egypt 12, Jan. 1985
Charles Ede Ltd, sale catalogue, *Small sculpture from Ancient Egypt*, London, 12, Jan. 1985
Smith, *Temple Production in the Middle Kingdom*
W. E. Smith, *Modeling the Mechanics of Temple Production in the Middle Kingdom: An Investigation of the Shena of Divine Offerings Adjacent to the Mortuary Temple of Senwosret III at Abydos, Egypt*, PhD Diss. (unpublished), University of Pennsylvania 2010.
Spanel, in: *Studies Simpson*
D. B. Spanel, 'Palaeographic and Epigraphic Distinctions between Texts of the So-called First Intermediate Period and the Early Twelfth Dynasty', in: *Studies in Honor of William Kelly Simpson*, ed. by P. Der Manuelian, Vol. II, Boston 1996, 765-786.
Steckeweh, *Die Fürstengräber von Qâw*
H. Steckeweh, *Die Fürstengräber von Qâw*, mit Beiträgen von Georg Steindorff/ und einem Anhang: Die griechisch-römischen Begräbnisstätten von Antaeopolis, von Ernst Kühn und Walther Wolf / mit einem Beitrag von Herman Grapow, Leipzig 1936
Stefanović, *The Title mr tA-mHw*
D. Stefanović, *The Title mr tA-mHw in the Middle Kingdom Documents*, Belgrade 2003.

Stefanović, in: *Art and Society*
D. Stefanović, '*sš ḳdwt*: the attestations from the Middle Kingdom and the Second Intermediate Period', in: K. A. Kóthay (ed.), *Art and Society. Ancient and Modern Contexts of Egyptian Art. Proceedings of the International Conference held at the Museum of Fine Arts, Budapest, 13-15 May 2010. Museum of Fine Arts*, Budapest 2012, 185-198.
Stefanović, *Regular Military Titles*
D. Stefanović, *The Holders of the Regular Military Titles in the Period of the Middle Kingdom: Dossiers*, London 2006.
Stefanović, *CdÉ* 85, 2010
D. Stefanović, 'The stela of wr-nTr at Saffron Walden Museum', *CdÉ* 85, 2010, 41-50
Stefanović, *CdÉ* 87, 2012
D. Stefanović, 'The Middle Kingdom Stela from the Toledo Museum of Art', *CdÉ* 87, 2012, 17-23.
Stefanović, in: *Acts of the X International Congress of Egyptologists*
D. Stefanović, 'Xkrt-nswt on the Monuments of ATw n Tt HqA' in:. *Acts of the X International Congress of Egyptologists*. Rhodes 2008 (forthcoming)
Stefanović, *SAK* 38, 2009
D. Stefanović, 'Stela Bolton 1920.10.12 – The Non-Royal Women of the Middle Kingdom II (Xkrt nswt, bAkt nt HqA, and anxt nt tpt nswt)', *SAK* 38, 2009, 297-309.
Stefanović, *SAK* 39, 2010
D. Stefanović, 'The Late Middle Kingdom stela of the staff of provisioning sector (Sna) (Musées d'art et d'histoire, Genève 6875)' *SAK* 39, 2010, 313-319, Taf. 30.
Stefanović, *GM* 213, 2007, 8-9.
D. Stefanović, 'A Note on the Stela Cairo SN 527', *GM* 213, 2007, 8-9.
Stefanović, *Journal of Classical Studies Matica Srpska* 12, 2010.
D. Stefanović, 'Stela London, British Museum EA 851', Stefanović, *Journal of Classical Studies Matica Srpska* 12, 2010, 59-62.
Stewart, *Egyptian Stelae* II
H. M. Stewart, *Egyptian Stelae, Reliefs and Paintings from the Petrie Collection. Part Two: Archaic to Second Intermediate Period*, Warminster 1979
Tallet, *GM* 193 (2003)
P. Tallet, 'The treasurer Ipi, early twelfth dynasty,' *GM* 193 (2003), 59-64
Tallet, in: *Studies Bourriau*
P. Tallet, 'Deux nouvelles stèles rupestres sur le plateau de Sérabit el-Khadim (Sud-Sinaï)', in: *Under the Potter's Tree. Studies in Ancinet Egypt Presented to Janine Bourriau on the Occasion of her 70th Birthday*, eds. D. Aston et al., Louven 2011, 933-948.

Тураев, *Записки Восточного отделения Императорского Русского археологического общества* 11, 1899

Б. А. Тураев, Описание египетских памятников в русских музеях и собраниях, *Записки Восточного отделения Императорского Русского археологического общества* 11, 1899, 115–164.

Tzachou-Alexandri, *The World of Egypt*

O. Tzachou-Alexandri, *The World of Egypt in the National Archaeological Museum,* Athens, 1995.

Valloggia, *BIFAO* 76, 1976

M. Valloggia, 'À propos du titre [oudjeb-oupout] « Économe »', *BIFAO* 76, 1976, 343-346

Vandekerckhove, Müller-Wollerman, *Die Felsinschriften des Wadi Hilâl*

H.Vandekerckhove et R.Müller-Wollerman, *Elkab VI. Die Felsinschriften des Wadi Hilâl*, Turnhout 2002

Verbovsek, *Private Tempelstatuen*

A. Verbovsek, *"Als Gunsterweis Des Königs in Den Tempel Gegeben…",* Private Tempelstatuen *Des Alten Und Mittleren Reiches*, ÄAT 63, Wiesbaden 2004.

Vercoutter, *Mirgissa* II

J. Vercoutter, *Mirgissa* II. *Les Nécropoles,* Paris 1975.

Vernus, *RdÉ* 26, 1974

P. Vernus, 'Une formule des shaoubtis sur un pseudonaos de la XIIIe dynastie', *RdE* 26, 1974, 100-114.

Vernus, *Surnom*

P. Vernus, *Le surnom au moyen empire*, Studia Pohl 13, Rome 1986

Vuilleumier – Chappaz, "*Sortir au jour*"

S. Vuilleumier – J-L. Chappaz, "*Sortir au jour*"*: art égyptien de la Fondation Martin Bodmer*, Cologny 2001.

Wegner, *JARCE* 35, 1998

J. Wegner, 'Excavations at the Town of Enduring-are-the-Places of Khakaure-Maa-Kheru-in-Abydos: A Preliminary Report on the 1994 and 1997 Seasons', *JARCE* 35, 1998, 1-44.

Wiedemann-Pörtner, *AG* III

A. Wiedemann – B. Pörtner, *Aegyptische Grab und Denksteine aus süddeutschen Sammlungen. Band 3: Bonn, Darmstadt, Frankfurt am Main, Genf, Neuchatel*, Strassburg 1906

Wild, *BIFAO* 69, 1970

H. Wild, 'Quatre statuettes du Moyen Empire dans une collection privée de Suisse', *BIFAO* 69, 1970, 89-130

Willems, *Chests of Life*

H. Willems, *Chests of Life*, Leiden 1988

Winlock, *JEA* 10, 1924

H.E. Winlock, 'The Tombs of the Kings of the Seventeenth Dynasty at Thebes', *JEA* 10, 1924, 217-227.

Winlock, *Rise and Fall*
H. E. Winlock, *The Rise and Fall of the Middle Kingdom of Thebes*, New York 1947.
Wozencroft, *GM* 213, 2007, 101-104
A. G. Wozencroft, 'A Scarab of the mid Thirteenth Dynasty attested to Redinptah', *GM* 213, 2007, 101-104.
Zitman, *Assiut*
M. Zitman, *The Necropolis of Assiut*, OLA 180, Leuven – Paris – Walpoe, MA 2010.
Žaba, *RILN*
Z. Žaba, *The Rock Inscriptions of Lower Nubia*, Prague 1974.

Dossier No. 1	*ꜥꜣm*
Mother:	Father: *nḥjj* (b-c)
Titles: *jmj-ḫt zꜣw pr* (a, c) *jmj-ḫt zꜣw* (b) *jmj-ḫt* (d)	Wife:

a. Inscription at Gebel Tjauti, Darnell, *Theban Desert Road Survey* I, 56 (GT 14).
b. Inscription at Gebel Tjauti, Darnell, *Theban Desert Road Survey* I, 57 (GT 15).
c. papyrus, Boulaq XVIII; Scharff, *ZÄS* 57, 1922, pl. 19**.
d. Inscription at Gebel Tjauti, Darnell, *Theban Desert Road Survey* I, 58 (GT 16).

Literature: Darnell, *Theban Desert Road Survey* I, 57.

Dating: 13th Dynasty

Dossier No. 2	*ꜥn*
Mother: *ḫwj*	Father:
Titles: *zꜣb r nḫn*	Wife: *nbt-pr zꜣt-jmn* (a)

a. stela, New York, MMA 69.30, Fischer, *Egyptian Studies* III, 123-129, pl. 21.
b. the lower part of a statue, New York, MMA, 1976.383, Fischer, *Egyptian Studies* III, 127-8 pl. 24 fig. 2.

Literature: Fischer, *Egyptian Studies* III, 127.

Dating: 13th Dynasty

Dossier Naro. 3	*ʿnḫ-jb*
Mother: *ddt-nbw* (a)	Father:
Titles: *ʿnḫ n nwt*	Wife:

a. stela, Leprohon, in: *Studies Simpson*, 523-531.
b. stela, Geneva D.51, Wiedemann-Pörtner, *AG* III, no. 3.

Literature: Stefanović, *Regular Military Titles*, no. 56.

Dating: 12th / 13th Dynasty

Dossier No. 4	*ʿnḫw*
Mother: *ḥnwt*	Father:
Titles: *wr mḏw šmʿw*	Wife:

a. stela, Cairo, CG 20724, Lange-Schäfer, *CCG* II, 353-355.
b. stela, Dreyer at al., *MDAIK* 64, 2008, 87.

Literature:

Dating: 13th / 17th Dynasty

Dossier No. 5	*ꜥnk.f*
Mother: *jw.s-n.(j)*	Father:
Titles: *jmj-r ẖmtjw jmj-jz* (a) *jmj-r pr wr jmj-jz* (b) *ẖtmtj-bjtj* (a, b) a. stela, Cairo, CG 20023, Lange-Schäfer, *CCG* II, 25-26. b. seals, Martin, *Seals*, nos. 345-347.	Wife:
Literature: Grajetzki, *Beamte*, 91 (III.20).	
Dating: 13th Dynasty (Neferhotep I)	

Dossier No. 6	*ꜥnkkw*
Mother:	Father:
Titles: *šmsw* a. seal, Martin, *Seals*, 348. b. inscription, Beni Hasan, tomb no. 3; Newberry, *Beni Hasan* I, pl. XXX.	Wife:
Literature: Stefanović, *Regular Military Titles*, no. 562.	
Dating: 12th Dynasty	

Dossier No. 7	*ʿpr-bʿ3rn*

Mother:	Father:
Titles: *jrj-pʿt, ḥ3ti-ʿ ḫtmtj-bjtj smr-wʿtj* (a) *jmj-r ḫtmt*	Wife:

a. door lintle, Abd el-Maksoud, *Tell Henoua*, 271-271, pl. 1.
b. offering stand, Berlin 22487, Krauss, *Orientalia* 62, 1993, 28, fig. 2; Ryholtt, *Second Intermediate Period*, 386, file 15.5, 8 (name only partly preserved).

Literature: Grajetzki, *Beamte*. 61 (II.28); Abd el-Maksoud, Valbelle, *RdE* 56 (2005), 11.

Dating: 15th Dynasty, Apophis Awoserre

Dossier No. 8	*ʿkj*

Mother: *nbt-pr mrw*	Father: *3ṯw n wḥmw w3ḏ*
Titles: *ḫtmtj-bjtj jmj-r ḫtmtjw sḏmj šnʿw* (c) *ḫtmtj-bjtj jmj-r ḫtmtjw sḏmj rmt* (b) *ḫtmtj-bjtj jmj-r wr* (d, e)	Wife:

a. stela, London, BM EA 210, *HTBM* V, pl. 14.
b. stela, Cairo, CG 20087, Lange-Schäfer, *CCG* II, 104-105 (= ANOC 19, pl. 29).
c. seal, Martin, *Seals*, 379.
d. seals, Martin, *Seals*, 371-378.
e. seal, Gratien, in: *Mélanges Vercoutter*, 98, pl. IV/6.

Literature: Franke, *Doss.*, 192 (a-d); Grajetzki, *Beamte*, 98 (III.36) (a-d)

Dating: 13th Dynasty

Dossier No. 9	*j3w-m-nwt*
Mother:	Father:
Titles: *wdpw*	Wife:

a. stela, Pittsburgh Acc.2983-6701; Patch, *Reflections of Greatness,* 33.
b. stela, Roanne 163; de Meulenaere, *CdE* LX, 119-120, 1985, 78, fig. 1.
c. stela, Dublin 1360; Quirke, *RdÉ* 51, 2000, 225-30, pl. XXXI.
d. stela, Chicago, Field Museum 31647; Allen, *Egyptian Stelae*, pl. VIII.

Literature: Grajetzki, *Two Treasurers*, 42.

Dating: 13th Dynasty (Sobekhotep II – Neferhotep I)

Dossier No. 10	*jjj*
Mother:	Father:
Titles: *ḫtmtj-bjtj sḏmj rmt jmj-r ḫmtjw* *ḫtmtj-bjtj jmj-r pr wr*	Wife:

a. scals, Martin, Seals, nos. 6, 1668.
b. seal, Martin, *Seals*, no. 4-5.

Literature: Grajetzki, *Beamte*, 94 (III.26).

Dating: 13th Dynasty

Dossier No. 11	*jjj*
Mother:	Father: *ḥrj ḫꜣwt mnṯw-ḥtp* (?)
Titles: *wr mḏw šmʿw*	Wife:

a. stela, Turin, Museo Egizio, Cat. 1582.
b. seal, Martin, *Seals*, no. 14.

Literature:

Dating: 13th Dynasty

Dossier No. 12	*jwjj*
Mother:	Father:
Titles: *ꜣṯw ʿꜣ n nwt*	Wife: *nbt-pr sꜣ-nt* (a)

a. stela, Cairo, CG 20304; Lange-Schäfer, *CCG* I, 316-317.
b. papyrus, Boulaq XVIII; Scharff, *ZÄS* 57, 1922, pl. 10**, 26.3.

Literature: Stefanović, *Regular Military Titles*, no. 277.

Dating: 13th Dynasty

Dossier No. 13	*jwjj*	
Mother: *rn.s-snb* (a)		Father: *ꜥnḫ n nwt jpw*
Titles: *šmsw šms* (a)		Wife:

a. stela, Cologny, Fondation Martin Bodmer 20, Vuilleumier – Chappaz, "*Sortir au jour*", 76-79, fig. 20.
b. stela, Rouen, Musée départemental des antiquités de la Seine-Maritime, Aeg. 348, Aufrère, *BIFAO* 85, 1985, 33-40, pl. 9.

Literature:

Dating: 13th Dynasty

Dossier No. 14	*jww*	
Mother: *nbt-pr ḥr-m-ḥb*		Father:
Titles: *jmj-r pr ḥsb jt*		Wife: *bbj*

a. stela, Museum of the Faculty of Letters, Kyoto University 36; Franke, *MDAIK* 57, 2001, 31-32.
b. stela, Habachi, *Heqaib*, 104, no. 87; K 8130 (find number); Franke, *MDAIK* 57, 2001, 25-30 (two fragments of one stela).

Literature: Franke, *MDAIK* 57, 2001, 30-32.

Dating: 13th Dynasty

Dossier No. 15	*jww*
Mother:	Father:
Titles: *jmj-ḫt z3w pr*	Wife: *ḥr-m-ḥb*

a. stela, Museum of the Faculty of Letters, Kyoto University 36 Franke, *MDAIK* 57, 2001, 31-32.
b. stela, Habaschi, *Heqaib*, 104, no. 87; K 8130 (fiind number); Franke, *MDAIK* 57, 2001, 25-30 (two fragments of one stela).

Literature:

Dating: 13th Dynasty

Dossier No. 16	*jw.f-n.j*
Mother:	Father:
Titles: *ʿnḫ n nwt*	Wife:

a. stela, Vienna, KHM ÄS 97; Hein – Satzinger, *Stelen des Mitleren Reiches* I, 5-8.
b. stela, London, BM EA 248; *HTBM* III, pl. 8.

Literature: Stefanović, *Regular Military Titles*, no. 9.

Dating: 12th / 13th Dynasty

Dossier No. 17	*jw-n.f*
Mother:	Father: *nḫt-ḫrw rn.f-snb* (b)
Titles: *ꜥḥꜥw* (a)	Wife:

a. stela, Toledo OH, Toledo Museum of Art, 1906.23, Stefanović, *CdE* 87, 2012, 17-23.
b. stela, Florence 6373, Bosticco, *Stele*, 55-56, no. 56.

[uncertain; based on stylistic similarities of the stelae' workshop]

Literature:

Dating: 13th Dynasty

Dossier No. 18	*jw-nfr*
Mother: *nbt-pr nḥjj*	Father:
Titles: *jmj-r jpt nswt*	Wife:

a. stela, Cairo, CG 20030, Lange-Schäfer, *CCG* I, 38-40.
b. stela, Vienna, KHM ÄS 172, Hein – Satzinger, *Stelen des Mitleren Reiches* II, 94-98.

Literature:

Dating: 13th Dynasty / Neferhotep I – Sebekhotep IV

Dossier No. 19	*jw-snb*
Mother: *nbt-pr w3ḏt-snb*	Father:
Titles: *zẖ3w n ẖnrt wr*	Wife:

a. stela, London BM EA 255, *HTBM* III, pl. 24.
b. pBoulaq 18, Scharff, *ZÄS* 57, 1922, pl. 7**, 20.16.

Literature: Quirke, *RdE* 39, 1988, 103.

Dating: 13th Dynasty (Sobekhotep II)

Dossier No. 20	*jw-snb*
Mother: *ẖmt-nn-sn* (a)	Father: *ḥ3t.j3w* (b)
Titles: *šmsw* (a) *šmsw n ḥḳ3* (b)	Wife:

a. statue, Habachi, *Heqaib*, 92-93, no. 68
b. stela, Vienna, KHM ÄS 175; Hein – Satzinger, *Stelen des Mitleren Reiches* I, 129-132

Literature: Stefanović, *Regular Military Titles*, nos. 493, 822.

Dating: 13th Dynasty

Dossier No. 21	*jbj*
Mother: *jpw* (a)	Father:
Titles: *wdpw* (a) *wdpw n ꜥt t* (b)	Wife:

a. stela, Vienna, KHM ÄS 9289; Hein – Satzinger, *Stelen des Mitleren Reiches* I, 177-179.
b. stela, Vienna, KHM ÄS 171; Hein – Satzinger, *Stelen des Mitleren Reiches* I, 124-128.

Literature:

Dating: 13th Dynasty

Dossier No. 22	*jb(.j)-jꜥw*
Mother: *nb ḥr-rdjt* ?	Father: *wsjr-mnḫ*
Titles: *zꜣb r nḫn*	Wife:

a. stela, Swansea University, Egypt Centre EC 7, Donohue, in: *Studies Malek*, 115-124, figs. 1-2.
b. stela, formerly Liverpool, World Museum 13.12.05.25, Donohue, in: *Studies Malek*, 126-127, figs. 3-4.

Literature: Donohue, in: *Studies Malek*, 119-120.

Dating: 13th Dynasty

Dossier No. 23	*jb(.j)-jꜥw*
Mother: *nb-ḥr-rdjt* ?	Father: *wsjr-mnḫ*
Titles: *zꜣb r nḫn* (b)	Wife:

a. stela, Swansea University, Egypt Centre EC 7, Donohue, in: *Studies Malek*, 115-124, figs. 1-2.
b. stela, formerly Liverpool, World Museum 13.12.05.25, Donohue, in: *Studies Malek*, 119, 126-127, figs. 3-4.

[Brother of above]

Literature: Donohue, in: *Studies Malek*, 119-120.

Dating: 13th Dynasty

Dossier No. 24	*jb(j)-jꜥ(w)*
Mother: (a) *zꜣt-ḥwt-ḥr*	Father: *sꜣb r nḫn wnmj* (a)
Titles: *smsw hꜣjjt*	Wife:

a. stela, Turin, Museo Egizio Suppl. 18130, Donadoni-Roveri, *Oriens Antiquus* 13, 1974, 53-56, pl. 3.
b. seal, Niccacci, *Scarabs*, no. 133, pl. 4.

[uncertain]

Literature: Ben-Tor, *BASOR* 294, 1994, 16 (59).

Dating: 13th / 17th Dynasty

<table>
<tr><td>Dossier No. 25</td><td colspan="2">jb.i-ꜥw-rs</td></tr>
<tr><td colspan="2">Mother:</td><td>Father: zẖꜣw n ẖnrt wr snb-n.j (a ?)</td></tr>
<tr><td colspan="2">Titles: zẖꜣw n ẖnrt (b)

a. stela, Edinburgh, Royal Museum of Scotland 1951.344, Fischer, Egyptian Titles, frontispiece.
b. stela, Cairo, CG 20322; Lange-Schäfer, CCG I, 334-335.

[uncertain]</td><td>Wife:</td></tr>
<tr><td colspan="3">Literature:</td></tr>
<tr><td colspan="3">Dating: 13th Dynasty</td></tr>
</table>

<table>
<tr><td>Dossier No. 26</td><td colspan="2">jbj-rs</td></tr>
<tr><td colspan="2">Mother:</td><td>Father:</td></tr>
<tr><td colspan="2">Titles: ꜣṯw ꜥꜣ n nwt

a. stela, Paris, Louvre E 17404.
b. stela, Aix-en-Provence, Musée Granet, 849-1-1S, Barbotin, Musée Granet, 46-49 [7].</td><td>Wife: zꜣ(t)-ḥtḥr (b)</td></tr>
<tr><td colspan="3">Literature:</td></tr>
<tr><td colspan="3">Dating: 13th Dynasty</td></tr>
</table>

Dossier No. 27	*jbj-jʿw*
Mother:	Father: *jnj-jtj.f* (d)
Titles: *ḥrj n tm* (a-c) *ḥrj n tm n nwt rsjt* (d)	Wife:

a. inscription Wadi el-Hol, Darnell, *Theban Desert Road Survey* I, 144 (WH 28)
b. inscription Wadi el-Hol, Darnell, *Theban Desert Road Survey* I, 145 (WH 29)
c. inscription Wadi el-Hol, Darnell, *Theban Desert Road Survey* I, 146 (WH 30)
d. seal, Cairo, JE 67371, Martin, *Seals*, 231.

Literature: Darnell, *Theban Desert Road Survey* I, 145.

Dating: 13th Dynasty

Dossier No. 28	*jb(j)-jʿ(w)*
Mother: *ḥ3-ʿnḫ.s* (a)	Father:
Titles: *šmsw* (a) *šmsw n rmn tp* (b)	Wife:

a. stela, Cairo CG 20255, Lange-Schäfer, *CCG* I, 274-275.
b. seal, Berlin 18162, Martin, *Seals*, 56.

Literature: Stefanović, *Regular Military Titles*, nos. 498, 802.

Dating: 13th Dynasty

Dossier No. 29	*jpj*
Mother: *jmjj* (b)	Father: *sbk-htp* (b)
Titles: *ḫtmtj-bjtj smr-wˁtj* *rḫ-nswt jmj-r pr sḏmj sḏmt* [*wˁ*], *jmj-r ḥwt*-[*wrt 6*] (a) *jrj-pˁt ḥ3tj-ˁ ḫtmtj-bjtj smr-wˁtj* *jmj-r ḫtmt* (b) a. coffin fragments, seen on the art market, Allen, in: *Theban Necropolis*, 19, n. 66. b. rock inscription, Ayn Soukhna, Abd el-Raziq et al., *Ayn Soukhna*, 47-49, no. 7.	Wife:
Literature: Grajetzki, *Two Treasurers*, 7; Allen, in: *Theban Necropolis*, 19-20; Tallet, *GM* 193, 2003, 59-64.	
Dating: Amenemhat I	

Dossier No. 30	*jpj*
Mother: *ṯtj*	Father:
Titles: *jrj-pˁt ḥ3tj-ˁ ḫtmtj-bjtj smr-wˁtj* *jmj-r rwjjt* c. statue, Hachachi, Heqaib, 88-89, no. 61. d. stela, Cairo CG 20288. e. tomb at Lisht (tomb C), Arnold, *Middle Kingdom Tomb Architecture*, 55-57.	Wife:
Literature: Franke, *Heqaib*, 55-56; Freed, in: *Studies Simpson* I, 327; Grajetzki, *Beamte*, 142 (VI.1).	
Dating: 12th Dynasty (Amenemhat II)	

Dossier No. 31	*jpj*
Mother: *mwt-ꜥnḫ* (b)	Father:
Titles:	Wife:

a. tomb of 'treasurer' *rḥw-r-ḏr.sn*, Arnold, *Middle Kingdom Tomb Architecture*, pl. 120a.
b. stela of 'treasurer' *rḥw-r-ḏr.sn*, New York MMA 12.182.1; Hayes, *Scepter of Egypt*, 333, fig. 221.

Literature:

Dating: 12th Dynasty (Amenemhat I?)

Dossier No. 32	*jpj-ꜥnḫw*
Mother:	Father:
Titles: *jmj-r šꜥtj* *ḫtmtj-bjtj* (b) *smr-wꜥtj* (b) *rḫ-niswt mꜣꜥ* (b) *mtj n zꜣ n mrj-kꜣ-rꜥ* (b) *ḫrp ꜥprw nfr* (b) *sḥḏ ḫntj-šj* (b)	Wife:

a. relief fragment, Firth, Gunn, *Teti Pyramid Cemeteries, I*, 208, no. 8.
b. coffin, Berlin 7796, *AIB* I, 130-132.

[both objects most likely from his tomb at Saqqara]

Literature:

Dating: 12th Dynasty (?)

Dossier No. 33	*jpw*
Mother:	Father:
Titles: *ˁnḫ n nwt*	Wife: *rn.s-snb* (a)

a. stela, Cologny, Fondation Martin Bodmer 20, Vuilleumier – Chappaz, "*Sortir au jour*", 76-79, fig. 20.
b. stela, Rouen, Musée départemental des antiquités de la Seine-Maritime, Aeg. 348, Aufrère, *BIFAO* 85, 1985, 33-40, pl. 9.

[his son *jwjj* is attested on both objects]

Literature: Stefanović, *Regular Military Titles*, nos. 22-23.

Dating: 13th Dynasty

Dossier No. 34	*jmjj*
Mother: *wḏ* (a)	Father:
Titles: *jmj-r pr* (b)	Wife: *jjj* (a)

a. stela, Cairo JE 36422, Baligh, *JARCE* 44, 2008,181-184.
b. stela, Brooklyn, Brooklyn Museum of Art 54.66, Spanel, in: *Studies Simpson* II, 772-777.

[uncertain]

Literature:

Dating: late 11th Dynasty

Dossier No. 35	*jmn-ꜥꜣ*
Mother:	Father:
Titles: *ꜥnḫ n nwt* (a) *ꜥnḫ n ṯt ḥḳꜣ* (b)	Wife:

a. stela, Cairo SN 527, Atallah, in: *Studies Radwan*, 151-158
b. seal, Martin, *Seals*, 175.

Literature: Stefanović, *GM* 213, 2007, 8-9.

Dating: 13th Dynasty

Dossier No. 36	*jmn-ꜥꜣ*
Mother: *ẖkrt-nswt wꜥtt snb.tj.sj*	Father:
Titles: *wr mḏw šmꜥw*	Wife:

a. stela, Turin, Museo Egizio Suppl. 18124.
b. stela, Tübinen, Ägyptologisches Institut der Universität Tübinen 462, Brunner-Traut – Brunner, *Sammlung der Universität Tübinen*, 84-85, Taf. 54 (Simpson, *ANOC* 60, pl. 42).

[Turin Suppl. 18124 is the third object of the ANOC 60; on the both stelae the *jmn-ꜥꜣ* is termed as *sn.f n mwt.f* → Franke, *AVB*, 133.

Literature:

Dating: 13th Dynasty

Dossier No. 37	*jmnjj*
Mother:	Father:
Titles: *jmj-r w*	Wife:

a. papyrus, London UC 32101H, Collier - Quirke, *Accounts*, 200-201.
b. ushabti, Paris, Louvre E 17221.

[uncertain]

Literature:

Dating: late 12th / 13th Dynasty

Dossier No. 38	*jmnjj*
Mother: *nbt-pr kmtt*	Father: *t-n-ḥꜥꜣw*
Titles: *jmj-r pr wr* *jrj-pꜥt, ḥꜣtj-ꜥ, ḫtmtj-bjtj* *wḏb-wpt*	Wife:

a. stela, Cairo, CG 20015, Lange-Schäfer, *CCG* I, 14-15.
b. stela, Cairo, CG 20101, Lange-Schäfer, *CCG* I, 122-123.
c. stela, Cairo, CG 20562, Lange-Schäfer, *CCG* II, 196-198.
d. statue, Petrie - Griffith, *Abydos* II, pl. XXIX, p. 34, 43.
e. Martin, *Seals*, 213-214.
f. stela in private collection, Roccati, in: *Legacy of Berlev*, 111-114, pl. 7.
g. stela in private collection, Roccati, in: *Legacy of Berlev*, 115-116, pl. 8.

[on stela f appears the *jmy-r ḫtmt snb-sw-ꜥ(.j)*, who is datable shortly before Neferhotep I; Grajetzki, *Two Treasurers*, 21]

Literature: Simpson, *ANOC* 10; Franke, *Doss.*, 98 (a-e).

Dating: late 13th Dynasty, Sobekhotep II – Neferhotep I (f)

Dossier No. 39	*jmnjj*
Mother:	Father:
Titles: *jmj-r ḥmw-nṯr*	Wife:

a. statue, Copenhagen, Ny Carlsberg Glyptotek, ÆIN 88, Koefoed-Petersen, *Stele eg. Copenhague*, 32 (55), pl. 65.
b. statue, New York, MMA 6.99.6, van Bothmer, *Ancient Art from New York Private Collections*, no. 66, pl. 20.

Literature: Mareé, in: *The Second Intermediate Period*, 270, n. 203.

Dating: 13th Dynasty

Dossier No. 40	*jmnjj*
Mother:	Father:
Titles: *jmj-r gnwtjw*	Wife: *z3t-ḥwt-ḥr* (b)

a. graffito, Abd el-Raziq et al., *Ayn Soukhna*, no. 14.
b. stela, Paris, Louvre C85, Fischer, *MMJ* 5, 1972, 20; Awad, *SAK* 39, 2010, 19-31, Taf. 1-2.

Literature:

Dating: late 12th / 13th Dynasty

Dossier No. 41	*jmnjj*
Mother: *nnj*	Father:
Titles: *wr mḏw šmꜥw*	Wife:

a. stela, Heqaib sanctuary, Habachi, *Heqaib*, no. 92.
b. stela, Vienna, KHM ÄS 103, Hein – Satzinger, *Stelen des Mitleren Reiches I*, 9-12.

[on both stelae appears a woman with the name *sn*(*t*)-*wrt*]

Literature: Franke, *Heqaib*, 67

Dating: 13th Dynasty

Dossier No. 42	*jmnjj*
Mother:	Father:
Titles: *ḫrp* (?) *ḥzww*	Wife:

a. statue, Jerusalem, Israel Museum 91.71.261, *Ancient Art. The Norbert Schimmel Collection*, no. 183.
b. coffin Lisht, LS 5115 H, Allen, *Coffin Texts*, 14, n. 29.

Literature:

Dating: late 12th Dynasty

Dossier No. 43	*jmnjj*
Mother: *ḏḥwtj-ḥtp* (?)	Father: Ukhhotep III, governor buried at Meir (b)
Titles: *z3-ḥ3tj-ʿ* (a)	Wife:

a. coffin New York, 11.150.39a, b, Kamal, *ASAE* 14, 1914, 56-57.
b. inscription, the tomb of his father Ukhhotep III at Meir, Blackman, *Meir* III, pl. XXVI.

Literature: Willems, *Chests of Life*, 88.

Dating: 12th Dynasty, about Senusret II/Senusret III

Dossier No. 44	*jmnjj*
Mother: *nbt-pr wḏ-ʿnḫ.s*	Father:
Titles: *smsw h3jjt*	Wife:

a. pBoulaq 18, Scharff, *ZÄS* 57, 1922, pl. 4**, 17.20
b. stela, Cairo CG 20086, Lange-Schäfer, *CCG* I, 101-103

Literature:

Dating: 13th Dynasty (Sobekhotep II)

Dossier No. 45 | *jmnjj / jj-jb-r.f* (b)

Mother: *z3t-sḥtp-jb-rʿ* Father:

Titles: *jmj-r pr* (b) Wife: *tnn* (a)

a. stela or rectangular slab, London, UC 14345, Stewart, *Egyptian Stelae* II, no. 115, pl. 29 [1].
b. rectangular slab, Los Angeles, Country Museum of Art, M.71.73.42.

Literature:

Dating: late 12th / 13th Dynasty

Dossier No. 46 | *jmnjj-snb*

Mother: *z3t-jʿḥ* (a) Father:

Titles: *jmj-r ḫtmt*
ḫtmtj-bjtj, smr wʿtj

a. stela, Petrie, *Tombs of Courtiers*, pl. XXVIII; Grajetzki, *Middle Kingdom*, pl. xx (Glasgow, Hunterian Museum).
b. seal, Gratien, *Prosopographie*, 39.

Literature: Grajetzki, *Beamte*, 55 (II.17)

Dating: late 12th / 13th Dynasty

Dossier No. 47	*jmnjj-snb*
Mother:	Father:
Titles: *jmj-r šnt*	Wife:

a. seal, Cairo, JE 58842, Martin, *Seal*, 223a
b. stela, Franke, in: *Die Pyramidenanlage des Königs Nub-Cheper-Re Intef*, fig. 27; Polz, in *Für die Ewigkeit geschaffen*, 20, fig. 22; Rummel, in: *Begegnung*, 32, no. 16.

Literature:

Dating: 13th Dynasty

Dossier No. 48	*jmnjj-snb*
Mother: *z3t-ṯnj*	Father: *ḥḳ3-jb*
Titles: *ḥ3tj-ʿ jmj-r ḥwt-nṯr*	Wife:

a. three statues, offering table, Habachi, *Heqaib*, 50-54, nos. 21-27.
b. stela, St. Petersburg, Hermitage, 1082, Bolshakov-Quirke, *Hermitage*, no. 7.
c. seal, von Pilgrim, *Untersuchungen*, no. 55 (Elephantine).
d. seal, London, BM EA 24107, Martin, *Seals*, 1558.
e. seal, London, UC 11376, Martin, *Seals*, 1559.
f. seal, Wegner, *JARCE* 35, 1998, 34-37 (19).

[a and c most likely identical, but the others?]

Literature: Franke, *Heqaib*, 41-42; see, Franke, *Doss.*, 122 (a-b)

Dating: late 12th /early 13th Dynasty

Dossier No. 49	*jmnjj-snb*
Mother:	Father:
Titles: *zẖ3w n ṯ3tj*	Wife:

a. seal, Wegner, *JARCE* 35, 1998, 39.
b. papyrus Brooklyn 35.1446, Hayes, *Papyrus of the Late Middle Kingdom*, recto column f.

Literature: Smith, *Temple Production in the Middle Kingdom*, 326.

Dating: late 12th / 13th Dynasty

Dossier No. 50	*jmn-m-ḥ3t*
Mother: *z3t-ṯnj*	Father:
Titles: *zẖ3w mšꜥ*	Wife:

a. offering table, London, BM EA 553, Habachi, *Heqaib*, no. 107.
b. altar and a pedestal, Habachi, *Heqaib*, 59-60, nos. 34-35.

Literature: Franke, *Heqai*b, 62-63; Stefanović, *Regular Military Titles*, no. 1104

Dating: end of 13th Dynasty

Dossier No. 51	*jmn-m-ḥ3t*

Mother: Father:

Titles: *jmj-r st* (a) Wife:
jmj-r st n ˁt t (b)

a. stela, Dublin 1360; Quirke, *RdÉ* 51, 2000, 225-230, pl. XXXI.
b. stela, Aberdeen, Anthropological Museum 1565, Ralston, in: *Legacy of Berlev*, 107-110, pl. 6.

[uncertain]

Literature:

Dating: 13th Dynasty

Dossier No. 52	*jmn-m-ḥ3t*

Mother: *nbt-pr z3t-ṯnj* (a) Father:

Titles: *wr mḏw šmˁw* Wife: *nbt pt nḫjjt* (b)

a. inscription, Petrie, *Season*, pl. VII, no. 159.
b. stela, Habachi, *Heqaib*, 102-103, no. 85.

Literature:

Dating: late 12th / 13th Dynasty

Dossier No. 53	*jmn-m-ḥ3t*
Mother: *w3ḏtt* ? (a)	Father:
Titles: *zẖ3w n ḏ3ḏ3t*	Wife:

a. inscription, Petrie, *Season*, pl. III, no. 86; *DeM*, 13 (no. 51).
b. inscription, Petrie, *Season*, pl. II, no. 69; *DeM*, 19 (no. 99).

Literature:

Dating: late 12th / 13th Dynasty

Dossier No. 54	*jmn-m-ḥ3t-snb*
Mother:	Father:
Titles: *smr, ḫrj-tp nswt, mḏḥ ḳdw nswt, ḥwt-ḥḏt, wr jrjjt m t3-wrt* (a)	Wife:

a. sarcophagus, Florence 2181, Bosticco - Rosati, *Aegyptus* 83, 2003, 15-52.
b. statue, Munich GL.97, Spiegelberg, *ZÄS* 65, 1930, 49, Taf. IVb.

[Identity uncertain, but several times proposed.]

Literature: Bosticco - Rosati, *Aegyptus* 83, 2003, 42; Fischer-Elfert - Grimm, *ZÄS* 130, 2003, 62, n. 13.

Dating: 12th Dynasty / Senwosret II or later

Dossier No. 55	*jmn-ḥtp*
Mother: *nfrw*	Father: *ḥ3tj-ʿ ḫtmw-nṯr ḥr*
Titles: *ḥ3tj-ʿ ḫtmw-nṯr*	Wife:

a. offering table, Cairo CG 23045, Kamal, *Tables d'offrandes*, 39-41.
b. stela, Cairo CG 20724, Lange-Schäfer, *CCG* II, 333-335.
c. steal, London UC 11345, Martin, *Seals*, no. 187.

[parents are known from the brother *snb-tjfj* (on b), Franke, 673)]

Literature: Sauneron, *BIFAO* 51, 1952, 156-158

Dating: early 13th Dynasty (?)

Dossier No. 56	*jn*
Mother: *nbt-pr nḫj*	Father: *ʿnḫ n nwt ʿnḫw*
Titles: *sḥḏ šmsw*	Wife:

a. stela, Copenhagen, Ny Carlsberg Glyptotek, ÆIN 964; Koefoed-Petersen, *Stele eg. Kopenhague*, no. 16; Jørgensen, *Catalogue Egypt I (3000-15500 B.C.)*, 190-191, no. 79.
b. stela, New York, MMA 68.14; Fischer, *Egyptian Studies III*, 129-130, pl. 25..

Literature: Stefanović, *Regular Military Titles*, no. 849.

Dating: 13th Dynasty / Sebekhotep II.

Dossier No. 57	*jnj-jtj.f*	
Mother: *snt* (a)		Father: *mrjj* (b)
Titles:		Wife:

a. inscription at Abd el Qadir (Lower Nubia), Hintze-Reineke, *FSN* I, 23-24, no. 5.
b. inscription at Abd el Qadir, Hintze-Reineke, *FSN* I, 33, mo. 51.
c. ushabti, Cairo, CG 46533, Newberry, *Funerary Statuettes*, 3.

Literature: Stefanović, *Regular Military Titles*, no. 1106.

Dating: end of 13th Dynasty

Dossier No. 58	*jnj-jtj.f*	
Mother:		Father:
Titles: *jmj-r bjtjw* *ẖrp rḫw-nswt* *jrj-pꜥt* (a) *ḥ3tj-ꜥ*		Wife:

a. stela, Cairo CG 20181, Lange-Schäfer, *CCG* I, 211.
b. seal, BM EA 3050, Martin, *Seals*, no. 234.

Literature: Grajetzki, *Beamte*, 189-190 (XII, 11).

Dating: 12th Dynasty / Senusret III, 14th year (a); the stela only names a king Senusret and not any other royal name, but Senusret III seems most likely, under him seals with names and titles started.

Dossier No. 59	*jnj-jtj.f*	
Mother: *ḥnwt.sn*		Father:
Titles: *ḥ3tj-ʿ*		Wife:

a. tomb, Bubastis no. 5.
b. mentioned on an offering table from Bubastis; Ahmed el Sawi, *ASAE* 63, 1979, 155-159, pls. III.

Literature: van Siclen, III, Schoske (editor), *Akten des vierten Internationalen Aegyptologischen Kongresses*, 193.

Dating: 12th /13th Dynasty

Dossier No. 60	*jnj-jtj.f*	
Mother: *ḥnwt.sn*		Father:
Titles: *ḥ3tj-ʿ, jmj-r ḥmw-nṯr*		Wife: *rn.f-ʿnḫ* (a) *z3t-ḥj* (b) *nbt-pr ḥm*[*t*] (c)

c. stela, Cairo CG 20064, Simpson, *ANOC* 33, pl. 51.
d. stela, Florence 2504, Simpson, *ANOC* 33, pl. 51.
e. stela, Paris, Louvre C313, Guichard, *RdE* 58, 2007, 222, pl. IVB.

Literature: Franke, *Doss.*, no. 143 (a-b); Stefanović, in: *Art and Society*, 193-194.

Dating: 12th Dynasty / Amenemhat III, year 37.(c)

Dossier No. 61	*jnj-jtj.f*
Mother: *snt*	Father:
Titles: *šmsw* (a) *šmsw n ḥḳ3* (b) a. inscription, Arkell, *JEA* 36, 1950, no. 2, 25. b. stela, Cairo, CG 20083; Lange-Schäfer, *CCG* I, 99.	Wife:
Literature: Stefanović, *Regular Military Titles*, no. 528; 825.	
Dating: 13th Dynasty	

Dossier No. 62	*jnpw*
Mother:	Father:
Titles: *ʿnḫ n nwt* a. inscription, Gasse-Randot, *Séhel*, SEH 194 (= *DeM* no. 118). b. inscription, Gasse-Randot, *Séhel*, SEH 195.	Wife:
Literature:	
Dating: 12th / 13th Dynasty	

Dossier No. 63	*jnpw-m-ḥ3t*
Mother:	Father:
Titles: *šmsw*	Wife:

a. stela, Cairo, CG 20372; Lange-Schäfer, *CCG* I, 374.
b. graffito, Arnold, *Control Notes*, 26 (E6).

Literature: Stefanović, *Regular Military Titles*, no. 539.

Dating: 12th Dynasty (Senusret I)

Dossier No. 64	*jntjj*
Mother:	Father:
Titles: *jmj ḫt z3w pr*	Wife: *ḥrj*

a. seal, Martin, *Seals*, 260.
b. stela in private collection, Roccati, in: *Legacy of Berlev*, 111-114., pl. 7

Literature: Roccati, in: *Legacy of Berlev*, 119.

Dating: 13th Dynasty (Neferhotep I and shortly before)

Dossier No. 65	*jzj*
Mother: *bjj* (a) / *nbt-pr bwjw* (b)	Father: *jbw* (b)
Titles: *rḫ-nswt* (a) *jmj-r ḫtmtjw šmsw-nswt* (b)	Wife:

a. stela Cairo, CG 20614, Lange-Schäfer, *CCG* II, 253-254.
b. stela, New York MMA 68.14; Fischer, *Egyptian Studies* III, 129-30, pl. 25.

Literature: Grajetzki, *Beamte*, 149 (VII, 10).

Dating: 13th Dynasty, about Neferhotep I (a)

Dossier No. 66	*jnj-jtj.f-ms*
Mother:	Father:
Titles: *z3-nswt*	Wife:

a. ushabti, Winlock, *Rise and Fall*, 134, pl. 47.
b. ushabti box, Winlock, *Rise and Fall*, 134, pl. 47.
c. statue, Manchester Museum 5051, Winlock, *JEA* 10, 1924, 218 n. 3.

Literature: Schmitz, *Königssohn*, 217-9, n. 2; Miniaci, in: *Il tempio e il suo personale nell'antico Egitto*, 113 (8).

Dating: 17th Dynasty

<table>
<tr><td>Dossier No. 67</td><td colspan="2">jn-ḥrt-ʿnḫ</td></tr>
<tr><td colspan="2">Mother:</td><td>Father:</td></tr>
<tr><td colspan="3">Titles: Wife: ḥpw (a) / ḥpjj (b)

a. stela, Тураев, Записки Восточного отделения Императорского Русского археологического общества 11, 1899, 147 (30)
b. stela, Sharpe, Egyptian Inscriptions II, 5, pl. 62.</td></tr>
<tr><td colspan="3">Literature:</td></tr>
<tr><td colspan="3">Dating: 13th Dynasty</td></tr>
</table>

<table>
<tr><td>Dossier No. 68</td><td colspan="2">w3ḥ-k3 (II)</td></tr>
<tr><td colspan="2">Mother: nbt-pr nfr-ḥtp</td><td>Father: jmj-r mrw ddw-sbk rn-nfr: jj-jb</td></tr>
<tr><td colspan="3">Titles: jmj-r ḥmw-nṯr Wife: ddt-sbk
ḥ3tj-ʿ

a. statue, Turin, Suppl. 4265, Melandri , Vicino. & Medio Oriente XV (2011), 249-270.
b. stela Turin Cat. No. 154, Steckeweh, Die Fürstengräber von Qâw, 47 (9), pl. 17a.
c. tomb 18 at Qaw el-Kebir; Steckeweh, Die Fürstengräber von Qâw, 48 (1-3) , pl. 10 c, d, p. 49 -52.

The statue Turin Suppl. 4265 was found in tomb 18 at Qaw el-Kebir; see now Melandri, Vicino & Medio Oriente XV, 2011, 250-252.</td></tr>
<tr><td colspan="3">Literature: Franke, Doss. 199 (a-b, identified as w3ḥ-k3 I and dated under Senusret III to Amenemhat III); Grajetzki, GM 156 (1997), 56-57 (identified as w3ḥ-k3 III).</td></tr>
<tr><td colspan="3">Dating: 12th Dynasty, about Senusret II – Senusret III</td></tr>
</table>

Dossier No. 69	*wj3w*
Mother: *ḥnwt* (a)	Father: *3ṯw n ṯt ḥḳ3 zj-n-wsrt* (b)
Titles: *zḥ3w mdḥw*	Wife:

a. seal, Martin, *Seals*, 402.
b. stela, Ballerini, *Bessarione* 7, 1910, 235-236 (i).

Literature:

Dating: 13th Dynasty

Dossier No. 70	*wp-w3wt-jrj*
Mother: *ẖkrt-nswt* ///// (e) ?	Father: *ẖtmtj-bjtj* ///*snb*/*rn.f-rs* (e) ?
Titles: *zḥ3w n ḥtpw nṯr*	Wife: *jrjt-pꜥt kwms*

a. stela, London, BM EA 833 + Laval, Museé du Vieux Château, 4560, Clère, *JEA* 68, 1982, 69-75, pl. 6.
b. stela, Cairo, CG 20335, Lange-Schäfer, *CCG* I, 349.
c. stela, Paris, Louvre C 287, Franke, *JEA* 71, 1985, 175-176, pl. 19
d. stela fragment, Liverpool Garstang Museum E.85.
e. stela fragment, Cairo, CG 20776, Lange-Schäfer, *CCG* II, 405-406.

Literature: Franke, *Doss.*, 204 (a-c); Mareé, in: *The Second Intermediate Period*, 272-273.

Dating: 13th Dynasty / Rahotep and later

Dossier No. 71	*wr-n(.j)-ptḥ*
Mother:	Father:
Titles: *jmj-r pr* (a) *jmj-r pr n jmj-r ḫtmt* (b)	Wife:

a. stela, Cairo, CG 20225, Lange-Schäfer, *CCG* I, 245.
b. stela, Rio de Janeiro, Museu Nacional 646 [2436], Kitchen, *Catalogue*, no. 18.

[*wr-n(.j)-ptḥ* was working for the *rḫ-nswt* (a) and later 'treasurer' *snbj*. *wr-n(.j)-ptḥ* became *jmj-r pr n jmj-r ḫtmt* when *snbi* was appointed 'treasurer'.]

Literature: Grajetzki, *Two Treasurers*, 42

Dating: Neferhotep I

Dossier No. 72	*wr-n(.j)-sbk*
Mother:	Father:
Titles: *jrj-ˁt n pr-ḥḏ* (a) *jmj-r st* (b)	Wife:

a. seal, London, UC 11439, Martin, *Seals*, 414.
b. stela, Marseille, Musée d'Archéologie méditerranéenne 227, Satzinger-Stefanović, in: *From Illahun to Djeme*, 243-245.

Literature: Satzinger-Stefanović, in: *From Illahun to Djeme*, 244-245.

Dating: late 12th / early 13th Dynasty

Dossier No. 73	*wr-ḫntj-ḫtjj*
Mother:	Father:
Titles: *jrj-ʿt* (a) *jmj-r pr* (b) a. stela, Cairo CG 20656, Lange-Schäfer, *CCG* II, 289. b. seal, Martin, *Seals*, 421 (found at Lahun). [uncertain] .	Wife:
Literature:	
Dating: 13th Dynasty	

Dossier No. 74	*wḫ-ḥtp*
Mother: *jt*	Father:
Titles: *wb3* a. stela, Paris, Louvre C187, Gayet, *Stèles de la XIIe dynastie*, 8, pl. XXXIX. b. statuette niche, Simpson, *Inscribed Materials*, 39, C7.	Wife:
Literature: Grajetzki, *RdE* 60, 2009, 214-216.	
Dating: 13th Dynasty	

Dossier No. 75	*wḫ-ḥtp*
Mother:	Father:
Titles: *jmj-r mšʿ*	Wife:

a. fragment of an diorite statue, Clèdat, *BIFAO* 1, 1901, 88.
b. inscription, Clèdat, *BIFAO* 2, 1902, 42 (9).

Literature: Stefanović, *Regular Military Titles*, no. 999.

Dating: 13th Dynasty

Dossier No. 76	*wsr*
Mother:	Father:
Titles: *jmj-r pr*	Wife:

a. seal, Cairo, JE 75208, Martin, *Seals*, 427.
b. stela, Paris, Louvre C308, Capart, *Monuments égyptiens* I, pl. XXVI.

Literature:

Dating: late 12th / 13th Dynasty

Dossier No. 77	*bbj*
Mother:	Father:
Titles: *ꜥnḫ n ṯt ḥḳꜣ* (a) *ꜣṯw n ṯt ḥḳꜣ* (b) a. stela, Sotheby's catalogue, N08500, New York 10 Dec 08. b. stela, Chicago, OIM E.6740, Garstang, *El-Arabah*, pl. XIII, E17.	Wife: *ḫkrt-nswt nbt-jwnt*
Literature: Mareé, in: *The Second Intermediate Period*, 267-268. pl 54; Stefanović, in: *Acts of the X International Congress of Egyptologists.*	
Dating: 13th Dynasty	

Dossier No. 78	*bbj*
Mother:	Father:
Titles: *wꜥb* a. stela, Bolton 20.10. 12, Stefanović, *SAK* 38, 2009, 297–309. b. stela, Cairo, CG 20724, Lange-Schäfer, *CCG* II, 353-355. c. stela, Nantes, Musée Dobreé E 13077, Andreau, *BSEG* 148, 2000, 25-26, fig. 5. [uncertain]	Wife: *rn.s-snb* (c)
Literature:	
Dating: 13th Dynasty	

Dossier No. 79	*p3-ntj-nj*
Mother: *nbt-pr jnj*	Father: *jḳr* (b,c)
Titles: *z3b sḥḏ zẖ3ww n nwt rsjt*	Wife: *nfrw-nbw* (a)

a. stela, London, BM EA 254, *HTBM* III, pl. 26.
b. stela, Paris, Louvre C 43, Hamza, *MDAIK* 63, 2007, 53-60, Taf.9.
c. stela, Rio de Janeiro, Museu Nacional 646 [2436], Kitchen, *Catalogue*, no. 18.

Literature: Franke, *Doss.* 231 (a-b); Grajetzki, *Two Treasurers*, 33.

Dating: 13th Dynasty

Dossier No. 80	*pwjwn*
Mother:	Father:
Titles: *jrj sdw*	Wife:

a. stela, London, BM EA 334, *HTBM* III, pl. 6.
b. stela, Saffron Walden Museum 1892.49, Stefanović, *CdE* 85, 2010, 41-50.

Literature: Franke, *Heqaib*, 76-77.

Dating: 13th Dynasty

Dossier No. 81	*ppj*
Mother:	Father:
Titles: *jmj-r ḥwt-nṯr* (a) *jmj-r ḥwt-nṯr n ḥḳ3t* (b)	Wife:

a. stela, Copenhagen Ny Carlsberg Glyptotek ÆIN 1540; Engelbach, *Harageh*, pls. XXIV, 2, LXXI; Jørgensen, *Catalogue Egypt I (3000-1550 B.C.)*, 164-165, no. 66.
b. papyrus, London, UC 32204; Collier - Quirke, *Letters*, 118-119.

Literature: Horváth, *Life and Afterlife*, 90.

Dating: late 12th Dynasty

Dossier No. 82	*m3*
Mother: *snn* (b)	Father: *ˁnkkw* (a)
Titles: *jmj-r 3ḥwt* (or *jmj-r w*)	Wife:

a. inscription, Beni Hasan, tomb 3, Newberry, *Beni Hassan* I, pl. XXX.
b. coffin Brussels E.5037 (BH1Br), Beni Hasan, tomb 500, Garstang, *Burial Customs*, 149, 192-93, 228, fig. 148, pl. IX.

Literature: Willems, *Chests of Life*, 66.

Dating: 12th Dynasty / Senusret II

Dossier No. 83	*m3ḥs-ḥtp*
Mother:	Father:
Titles: *ḥ3tj-ꜥ*	Wife:

a. tomb no. 3 at Bubastis.
b. statue base, found at the palace at Bubastis.

Literature: van Siclen, III, in: S. Schoske (editor), *Akten des vierten Internationalen Aegyptologischen Kongresse*, 192.

Dating: 12th Dynasty

Dossier No. 84	*mmj*
Mother:	Father:
Titles: *wꜥb*	Wife:

a. stela, Chicago, Field Museum of Natural History A.31649, Allen, *Egyptian Stelae*, 16-17, pl. IV.
b. offering table, Cairo, CG 23045, Kamal, *Tables d'offrandes* I, 39-41.

Literature:

Dating: late 12th / 13th Dynasty

Dossier No. 85	*mnw-ḥtp*
Mother: *nbt-pr mmj*	Father:
Titles: *jmj-r pr*	Wife:

a. stela, Cambridge, Fitzwilliam Museum E.51.1901, Martin, *Stelae*, no. 18.
b. statuette, London UC14752, Page, *Egyptian sculpture*, no. 139.

Literature:

Dating: late 12th Dynasty

Dossier No. 86	*mnṯw-ꜥꜣ*
Mother: *ḥpw* (b)	Father:
Titles: *ḥm-nṯr* (a) *ḥm-nṯr ꜥꜣ* (b)	Wife: *nbt-pr ṯt* (b)

a. stela, London, UC 14435, Stewart, *Egyptian Stelae* II, no. 53, pl. 11 [3].
b. stela, Leiden, Rijksmuseum van Oudheden AP. 20, Boeser, *Leiden*, 51, pl. 39.

Literature:

Dating: 12th Dynasty

Dossier No. 87	*mnṯw-m-ḥb*
Mother:	Father:
Titles: *r nḫn* (a) *z3b r nḫn* (b) *wr mḏw šmʿw* (c)	Wife:

a. stela, Brussels, Musée Royaux d'Art et d'Histoire E.480, Mareé, in: *The Second Intermediate Period*, 247, pl. 86.
b. stela, London BM EA 362, *HTBM* III, pl. 39.
c. stela, Athens, National Archaeological Museum 4054, Tzachou-Alexandri, *The World of Egypt*, no. 22.

[uncertain]

Literature: Mareé, in: *The Second Intermediate Period*, 275.

Dating: 13th Dynasty

Dossier No. 88	*mnṯw-ḥtp*
Mother: *nfrt-tw*	Father:
Titles: *jmj-r pr ḥsb jt* (a) *jmj-r ḥmw-nṯw* (b)	Wife:

a. stela, London, BM EA 187, *HTBM* II, pl. 13.
b. stela, London, BM EA 210, *HTBM* II, pl. 34.

Literature:

Dating: late 12th / 13th Dynasty

Dossier No. 89	*mnṯw-ḥtp*	
Mother: *nbr pr snt*		Father: *ꜥnḫ n nwt ꜥnḫw*
Titles: *sḥḏ šmsw*		Wife:

a. stela, New York, MMA 63.154; Fischer, *Egyptian Studies* III,130-133, pl. 26.
b. stela, Copenhagen, Ny Carlsberg Glyptotek, ÆIN 964; Koefoed-Petersen, *Stele eg., Copenhague*, no. 16; ; Jørgensen, *Catalogue Egypt I (3000-15500 B.C.)*, 190-191, no. 79.

Literature: Stefanović, *Regular Military Titles*, no. 862.

Dating: 13th Dynasty / Sebekhotep II

Dossier No. 90	*mrr*	
Mother:		Father:
Titles: *jmj-r šnt*		Wife:

a. inscription, Gebel Tjauti, Darnell, *Theban Desert Road Survey* I, 61 (GT 18).
b. inscription, Gebel Tjauti, Darnell, *Theban Desert Road Survey* I, 62 (GT 19).
c. inscription, Gebel Tjauti, Darnell, *Theban Desert Road Survey* I, 62 (GT 20).
d. inscription, Gebel Tjauti, Darnell, *Theban Desert Road Survey* I, 63 (GT 21).

Literature:

Dating: 13th / 17th Dynasty

Dossier No. 91	*msḫt*	
Mother: *ḥwt-hrw* (b)		Father: *ẖtjj*
Titles: *jmj-r ꜥẖnwtj* (a, b) *jmj-r tꜣ-mḥw* (b)		Wife:

a. canopic Box; London BM EA 46638; Lüscher, *Kanopenkästen*, 5, 51-52, 100 (no. 26), pl. 12; Zitman, *Assiut* II, 135 (S74L).
b. stela, Leiden, Rijksmuseum van Oudheden AP. 69, Boeser, *Leiden*, 41, pl. 31.

[uncertain; the name on the Leiden stela could be also read as *sbktj*]

Literature: Zitman, *Assiut* II, 182

Dating: late 12th Dynasty

Dossier No. 92	*mkt*	
Mother: *ptrw* (a)		Father:
Titles: *jmj-r pr*		Wife:

a. stela, Cairo CG 20080, Lange-Schäfer, *CCG* I, 96-97.
b. graffito, Abd el-Raziq et al., *Ayn Soukhna*, 49, no. 8.

Literature:

Dating: 12th Dynasty

Dossier No. 93	*mkt-ꜥnḫw*	
Mother: *zꜣt-ppjj-jdw* (?)		Father:
Titles: *jmj-r pr wr* *ḫtmtj-bjtj smr-wꜥtj* *jrj-pꜥt ḥꜣtj-ꜥ* (a) a. inscription, Petrie, *Season,* pl. 3, no. 81. b. stela Cairo JE 91283 (Abydos), Simpson, *Inscribed Material,* 36-39, C4. fig. 61, pl. 7.		Wife:
Literature: Franke, *Heqaib,* 62; Grajetzki, *Beamte*, 87 (III.14)		
Dating: 12th Dynasty / Amenemhat III, year 4		

Dossier No. 94	*nj-sw-mnṯw*	
Mother:		Father:
Titles: *ḥꜣtj-ꜥ* a. stela, London, UC 14551, Stewart, *Egyptian Stelae* II, 29, pl. 31/4. b. offering table, Vienna, KHM ÄS 98, *Götter*, *Menschen*, *Pharaonen,* no. 69.		Wife:
Literature:		
Dating: 12th Dynasty		

Dossier No. 95	*nj-sw-mnṯw*	
Mother: *mrjjt*		Father:
Titles: *jrj-pꜥt, ḥ3tj-ꜥ, ḫtmtj-bitj,* *smr-wꜥtj, rḫ-nswt* *jmj-r ḥmw-nṯr* (a) *ḥ3tj-ꜥ, jmj-r ḥmw-nṯr* (b-c)		Wife:

a. stela, Paris, Louvre C243, Fischer, *RdE* 24, 1972, 70, pl. 7B.
b. stela, Cairo, CG 20733, Lange-Schäfer, *CCG* II, 363-365
c. Vienna, KHM ÄS 5786, Jaroš-Deckert, *Statuen*, 60-63.

Literature: Franke, *Doss.,* 283 (a-b).

Dating: 12th Dynasty / Amenemhat II – Senusret III

Dossier No. 96	*nwb-k3w-rꜥ*	
Mother:		Father:
Titles: *ḥ3tj-ꜥ*		Wife:

a. ostracon, OG 6, Mahfouz, *Afrique & Orient* 41, 2006, 33.
b. Papyrus from Lahun, Berlin 10012, Borchardt, *ZÄS* 37, 1899, 89-103.

Literature: Mahfouz, *Afrique & Orient* 41, 2006, 32.

Dating: 13th Dynasty

Dossier No. 97	*nwb-k3w-rʿ-ʿnḫ*
Mother:	Father:
Titles: *wr m33w m jwnw* *jrj-pʿt, ḥ3tj-ʿ*	Wife:

a. offering stand, Gabrab - Nagib, *Varia Aegyptiaca* 10 (2-3), 1995, 101-104.
b. rock inscription, Engelbach - Townsend, *ASAE* 33, 1933, 1-5.

Literature: Grajetzki, *Court Officials*, 177

Dating: 12th Dynasty

Dossier No. 98	*nbww*
Mother: *jjt*	Father:
Titles: *wr mḏw šmʿw*	Wife:

a. base of seated statuette, London UC 14727, Page, *Egyptian Sculpture*, no. 147.
b. seal, Martin, *MDAIK* 35, 1979, 221 (42).

Literature:

Dating: 13th Dynasty

Dossier No. 99	*nbw-m-sn.j*
Mother:	Father:
Titles: *r nẖn* (a) *jmj-r ḥsw, wr mḏw šmʿw* (b)	Wife: *mrrjj* (a)

a. stela, Ithaca, Cornell University – Anthropology Collections 967.3.75, Mareé, in: *The Second Intermediate Period*, 246 (z), pl. 79.
b. stela, Toulouse, Musée Georges Labit 49.277, Ramond, *Musée Labit*, no. 5, pl. V.

[uncertain]

Literature: Mareé, in: *The Second Intermediate Period*, 274-275.

Dating: 13th / 17th Dynasty

Dossier No. 100	*nb-pw*
Mother:	Father: *sḥtp-jb-rʿ* (b)
Titles: *ʿnẖ n nwt*	Wife:

a. inscription, Gasse-Randot, *Séhel*, SEH 196 (= *DeM* no. 128).
b. inscription, Petrie, *Season*, pl. X, no. 270 (= *DeM* no. 166).

Literature: Stefanović, *Regular Military Titles*, no. 98.

Dating: 13th Dynasty

Dossier No. 101	*nb-swmnw*
Mother:	Father:
Titles: *ḫtmtj-bjtj, jmj-r ḫtmtjw, sḏmj šnꜥ* (a) *ḫtmtj-bjtj, jmj-r ḫtmtjw* (b)	Wife:

a. seal, Cairo JdE 75082, Martin, *Seals*, 1118.
b. stela, Madrid 1999/99/4, Meeks, *ENIM* 2, 2009, 129-154.

Literature: Ryhold, *Second Intermediate Period*, 358 (File 13/55, no. 2); Grajetzki, in: *The Second Intermediate Period*, 306.

Dating: 13th Dynasty / *sḫꜥ-n-rꜥ sꜥnḫ-ptḥ*

Dossier No. 102	*nb-swmnw*
Mother: *nbt-pr jtj* (a-b)	Father:
Titles: *jrj-ꜥt n ꜥt ḥnḳt*	Wife:

a. stela, Louvre E.20002, Moret, *Stèles*, 25-29 (C12).
b. inscription, Petrie, *Season*, pl. X, no. 270.
c. seal, Aberdeen, Martin, *Seals*, 675.
d. seal, Jerusalem, Israel Museum 76.31.84, Ben-Tor, *IMJ* 8, 1988, 38 (6).

Literature: Franke, *Doss.*, 300 (a-c).

Dating: 13th Dynasty

Dossier No. 103	*nmtj-ḥtpw*
Mother:	Father:
Titles: *jmj-r pr* (a) *ḫtmtj-bjtj, jmj-r pr wr,* *šmsw nsw* (b)	Wife:

a. statue, Berlin, ÄM 15700, Lembke, *GM* 150, 1996, 81-86.
b. seal, New York, MMA 22.2.245, Martin, *Seals*, 360.

[uncertain]

Literature:

Dating: 13th Dynasty

Dossier No. 104	*nfr-jw*
Mother: *nbt-pr prt* (a)	Father: *sḥtp-jb* (b)
Titles: *ḫtmw kf3 jb*	Wife: *prr* (a)

a. inscription near Kumna (Lower Nubia), Hintze-Reineke, *FSN* I, 140, no. 487.
b. Inscription near Kumna, Hintze-Reineke, *FSN* I, 127, no. 453.

Literature:

Dating: 12th / 13th Dynasty

Dossier No. 105	*nfr-ḥtp*
Mother: *nbt-pr ẖmt-sm-jb* (a)	Father: *jmj-r pr ḥsb jt nb-swmnw* (a)
Titles: *ꜥḥꜥ*	Wife: *nbt-pr rn.s-rs* (b)

a. stela, London, BM EA 930, *HTBM* IV, pl. 41.
b. stela, Berlin 7300, *AIB* I, 188-189.

Literature:

Dating: 13th Dynasty

Dossier No. 106	*nfr-ḥtp*
Mother:	Father:
Titles: *wr mḏw šmꜥw*	Wife:

a. stela, Turin, Museo Egizio Suppl. 18124.
b. stela, Tübinen, Ägyptologisches Institut der Universität Tübinen 462, Brunner-Traut – Brunner, *Sammlung der Universität Tübinen*, 84-85, Taf. 54 (Simpson, *ANOC* 60, pl. 42).

Literature:

Dating: 13th Dynasty

Dossier No. 107	*nḥjj*
Mother: *snb* (a)	Father:
Titles: *z3b r nḫn*	Wife:

a. rock inscription at Hieraconpolis, Darnell, Darnell, *Nekhen News*, Fall 1996 (8), 6-7.
b. stela London UC 14418, Steward, *Egyptian Stelae II*, no. 113, pl. 28.3.

[uncertain; on the stela appears also an *3ṯw n ṯt ḥḳ3 rn-snb* (Franke, Doss. 360) also known from a rock inscription at Hieraconpolis; Darnell, *JARCE* XXXVI, 1999, 23-25]

Literature: Darnell, Darnell, *Nekhen News*, Fall 1996 (8), 6-7.

Dating: 13th Dynasty

Dossier No. 108	*nḥjj*
Mother: *snb* (a)	Father:
Titles: *jmj-r st* (a) *jmj-r st n ʿt jrṯt* (b)	Wife:

a. stela, Liverpool, World Museum M13635, Grajetzki, *Two Treasurers*, 28-29, pl. 2.
b. stela, Oldenburg, Landesmuseum Natur und Mensch 4403, Franke, *SAK* 10, 1983, 157-178, Taf. I.

[uncertain]

Literature:

Dating: 13th Dynasty / Neferhotep I - Sebekhotep IV

Dossier No. 109	*nḥjj-snbj*
Mother: *jwj* (a)	Father:
Titles: *jmj-pr wr* *ḫtmtj-bjtj* *wḏb wpt* (c, d)	Wife:
a. inscription, Petrie, *Season*, pl. IX, no. 267 (as *jmn-m-ḥ3t nḥjj-snbj*). b. seals, BM EA 64854, Cambridg, Fitzwilliam E. 96.1920; Moscow 2305, Martin, *Seals*, no. 774-777. c. seals, New York MMA. 26.7.274; Martin, *Seals*, no. 778-779. d. statue, Valloggia, *BIFAO* 76, 1976, 344, no. 8 (as *jmn-m-ḥ3t nḥjj-snbj*).	
Literature: Valloggia, *BIFAO* 76, 1976, 344, nos. 8-9; Vernus, *Surnom*, 8-9, no. 22; Grajetzki, *Beamte*, 97 (III, 33).	
Dating: late 12th/ 13th Dynasty	

Dossier No. 110	*nḥrj*
Mother: *t3t*	Father: *ḫnmw-ḥtp* (II)
Titles: *z3-ḥ3ty* (b)	Wife:
a. stela, Oxford Ashmolean Museum E.3987; Garstang, *Burial customs,* 187, fig. 195; Grajetzki, *Court Officials*, fig. 57. b. inscription, Beni Hasan, tomb no. 3; Newberry, *Beni Hasan I*, pl. XXXV. [Son of the local governor Khnumhotep II, tomb 3 at Beni Hasan]	
Literature: Grajetzki, *Court Officials*, 137-139, figs. 54, 57.	
Dating: 12th Dynasty, Senusret II-Senusret III	

Dossier No. 111	*nḫt*
Mother: *z3t-ḥwt-ḥrw*	Father:
Titles: *jmj-r pr wr* (b) *jmj-r pr* (c, d) *jmj-r ḫtmt* ? (a) *ḫtmtj-bjtj* (c) *jrj-pꜥt, rḫ-nswt m3ꜥ* (d) a. tomb 493 at Lisht, Arnold, *Middle Kingdom Tomb Architecture,* 72-75, pl. 146a. b. statue from his tomb, Cairo CG 409, Borchardt, *Statuen und Statuetten*, 20-21. c. control note, Arnold, *Control Notes,* 110, no. N19. d. statue, Naples Museo Archeologico Nazionale 983, *Collezione Egiziana di Napoli*, 42 (1.4).	Wife:
Literature: Franke, *Heqaib*, 58, n. 179; Arnold, *GM* 122, 1991, 78; Grajetzki, *Beamte*, 82-83 (III.5).	
Dating: 12th Dynasty / Senusret I, around year 12 (c)	

Dossier No. 112	*nḫt*
Mother:	Father:
Titles: *jmj-r st n ꜥt dḳr* a. stela, Vienna, KHM ÄS 181, Hein – Satzinger, *Stelen des Mitleren Reiches* I, 133-136. b. stela, Toulouse, Musée G. Labit 49.267, Ramond, *Musée Labit*, 1-3.	Wife:
Literature: Grajetzki, *Two Treasurers*, 70.	
Dating: 13th Dynasty / Sebekhotep III	

Dossier No. 113	*nḫt*
Mother:	Father:
Titles: *jmj-r gs-pr*	Wife:

a. statuette, Toronto, Royal Ontario Museum 905.2.79, Mareé, in: *The Second Intermediate Period*, 246 (v), pls. 74-75.
b. statue, Moscow, Pushkin State Museum of Fine Arts I.1.a.5731, Berlev-Hodjash, *Sculpture of Ancient Egypt*, no. 31.

Literature: Mareé, in: *The Second Intermediate Period*, 274.

Dating: 13th Dynasty

Dossier No. 114	*nḫt*
Mother: *snb///* (b)	Father:
Titles: *ꜥḥꜣwtj*	Wife:

a. coffin fragments, Fitzwilliam Museum Cambridge E.216.1903, Garstang, *Burial customs*, pl. VII, 217.
b. stela, Paris, Louvre C171, Gayet, *Stèles de la XIIe dynastie*, 11 (as C45).

Literature:

Dating: late 12th/ 13th Dynasty

Dossier No. 115	*nḫtj*		
Mother:	*nntt-b3w* ?	Father:	
Titles: *jmj-r t3-mḥw*		Wife:	

a. offering table, Cairo JdE 91220, Simpson, *Inscribed Materials*, C15, fig. 72
b. ushabti, Ashmolean Museum, E.2128, Garstang, *El-Arabah*, 5, 32; Pls. III, XV.

Literature: Stefanović, *The Title mr t3-mḥw,* 34.

Dating: late 12th/ 13th Dynasty

Dossier No. 116	*nḫtj*		
Mother:		Father:	
Titles: *ḥ3tj-ʿ, ḥrj-tp ʿ3 n zp3t*		Wife:	

a. tomb no. 21, Beni Hasan, Newberry, *Beni Hasan* II, 26, pl. XXII-XXIIa.
b. inscription, tomb 3, Beni Hasan, Newberry, *Beni Hasan* II, pl. XXV, 54.

Literature:

Dating: 12th Dynasty, Senusret I

Dossier No. 117	*nḫtj*
Mother:	Father:
Titles: *ḥ3tj-ꜥ*	Wife:

a coffin lid, Turin Prov. 1565, Leospo, Enrichetta, in Donadoni Roveri, *Passato e futuro del Museo Egizio di Torino (Archivi di Archeologia).*

a. fragment of offering table, Turin Suppl. 22019; Habachi, *Tavole d'offerta are e bacilli da libagione*, 25-26.

b. stela, Stockholm MM 32004; Steckeweh, *Die Fürstengräber von Qâw*, 8 (uncertain).

[father of *w3h-k3* (c), governor at Qaw el-Kebir, not *w3ḥ-k3* II]

Literature: Steindorff, in: Steckeweh, *Die Fürstengräber von Qâw*, 48; Grajetzki, *GM* 156, 1997, 59.

Dating: late 12th Dynasty, about Senusret II/Senusret III

Dossier No. 118	*nḫtj*
Mother: *trt* (b)	Father:
Titles: *zẖ3w n w* (a) *zẖ3w n ḳnbtj n w* (b)	Wife: *nbt-pr ḥnwjj* (a)

a. stela, London, BM EA 851, Stefanović, *Journal of Classical Studies Matica Srpska* 12, 2010, 59-62.

b. lower part and base of statuette, London, UC 14652, Page, *Egyptian Sculpture*, no. 35.

Literature: Russo, *Territory w*, 48 (b).

Dating: 13th / 17th Dynasty

Dossier No. 119	*nṯr-jsj*
Mother:	Father:
Titles: *z3b r nḫn*	Wife:

a. Shatt er-Rigal, graffito, Winlock, *Rise and Fall*, 72, pl. 39 III.
b. statuette, Leipzig 1023, Krauspe, *Statuen und Statuetten*, 62-63, pls. 54-55.

[uncertain identification with *wr mḏw šmʿw nṯr-jsj* attested on stela Cairo TR 9/6/18/27. See Mareé, in: *The Second Intermediate Period*, 275, n. 239]

Literature: Mareé, in: *The Second Intermediate Period*, 275, n. 239.

Dating: 13th Dynasty

Dossier No. 120	*n-snt-jb*
Mother:	Father:
Titles: *jmj-r nbjw*	Wife:

a. seal, Jerusalem, Israel Museum 76.31.69, Ben-Tor, *Scarab*, no. 11.
b. seal, Martin, *Seals*, 631.

Literature:

Dating: 13th Dynasty

Dossier No. 121	*nṯnw*
Mother:	Father:
Titles: *jdnw n jmj-r ḫtmt*	Wife:

a. seal, Los Angeles, County Museum of Art M.86.313.8, Cooney - Tyrrell, *PalArch's Journal of Archaeology of Egypt/Egyptology* 4,1.2, 2005, 75.
b. seal, Cairo, JE 75943, Martin, *Seals*, 1741.

Literature:
Dating: 13th Dynasty

Dossier No. 122	*nṯr(j)-pw / gbw*
Mother: *nt-jb*	Father: *wḥmw*
Titles: *ꜣṯw ꜥꜣ n nwt*	Wife:

a. inscription near Kumna, Hintze-Reineke, *FSN* I, 144, no. 496.
b. inscription near Kumna, Hintze-Reineke, *FSN* I, 145, no. 497.

Literature: Vernus, *Surnom*, no. 143, 34; Stefanović, *Regular Military Titles*, no. 287.
Dating: 12th Dynasty / Amenemhat III

Dossier No. 123 | *nṯrw-ḥtp*

Mother:

Father: *ẖnmw-ḥtp* (b)

Titles: *jmj-r pr* (a, b)
jmj-r pr ḏꜣḏꜣt (b)
zẖꜣw (a)

Wife:

a. coffin (BH4C), Cairo JE 37565.
b. inscription, tomb no. 3, Beni Hasan, Newberry, *Beni Hasan I*, pl. XXIX, XXXV.

Literature: Willems, *Chests of Life*, 66.

Dating: 12th Dynasty, Senusret II (b)

Dossier No. 124 | *rꜥ-msw*

Mother: *zꜣt-ḥꜣtj-ꜥ ꜣst*

Father:

Titles: *ꜣṯw n ṯt ḥḳꜣ*

Wife: *ẖkrt nswt nfrt-wbn.s*

a. stela, Cairo JE 46785, Engelbach, *ASAE* 23, 1923, 183-186.
b. stela, Cairo JE 48229, Marée, *BMSAES* 12, 2009, 60-62, fig. 17.

both stelae found at Edfu

Literature: Stefanović, *Regular Military Titles*, no. 428 (a); Marée, *BMSAES* 12, 2009, 60-62.

Dating: 13th Dynasty

Dossier No. 125	*rꜥ-msw*
Mother: *ẖkrt-nswt nfrt-wbn.s*	Father: *zꜣ-nswt ḥr-ḫw.f*
Titles: *ꜣṯw n ṯt ḥkꜣ* (a) *zꜣ-nswt* (b) a. stela, Cairo JE 48229, Marée, *BMSAES* 12, 2009, 60-62, fig. 17. b. stela, Marée, *Afrique & Orient* 53 2009, 11-21, figs. 2-3.	Wife:
Literature: Marée, *Afrique & Orient* 53 2009, 11-21; Miniaci, in: *Il tempio e il suo personale nell'antico Egitto*, 122 (37).	
Dating: 13th / 17th Dynasty	

Dossier No. 126	*rꜥ-stẖ*
Mother: *kms-n.j*	Father: *nfr-jw*
Titles: *ẖtmw kfꜣ jb* (a) *ẖtmw kfꜣ jb n ẖrp kꜣt* (b) a. stela, London, BM EA 224, *HTBM* III, pl. 17. b. offering table, Reggio Emilia 1; Pernigotti, *Antichità egiziane del Museo Gaetano Chierici*, pl. 1.	Wife:
Literature: Quirke, *RdÉ* 51, 2000, 232, n. 33 (on the name and title)	
Dating: 12th /13th Dynasty	

Dossier No. 127	*rn.f-snb*
Mother:	Father:
Titles: *jrj-ꜥt n pr ḥ* (a) *jrj-ꜥt* (b)	Wife:

a. fragment of an statuette, Giveon, *IEJ* 34, 1984, 154-155 pl. 19 fig. 1.
b. inscription, Černy, *IS* no. 90.

Literature:

Dating: 12th Dynasty / Amenemhat III

Dossier No. 128	*rnpjj.f* / *rnpt*
Mother:	Father:
Titles: *jmj-r st* *jmj-r st n jmj-r ḫtmt* (c)	Wife: *jḥj* (d), *jtj* (a, b, c)

a. stela, Pittsburgh Acc. 2983-6701; Patch, *Reflections*, 33.
b. stela, London BM EA 252; *HTBM* III, pl. 46 (ANOC 25.2).
c. stela, Dublin UC 1360, Quirke, *RdÉ* 51, 2000, 225-30, pl. XXXI.
d. stela, London BM EA 240; *HTBM* II, pl. 32.

[worked under the 'treasurer' *snb-sw-mꜥ.j*, Grajetzki, *Two Treasurers*, 21]

Literature: Quirke, *RdÉ* 51, 2000, 225-230; Grajetzki, *Two Treasurers*, 43; Grajetzki, *Court Officials*, fig. 50.

Dating: 13th Dynasty, about Sobekhotep II to Neferhotep I

Dossier No. 129	*rn-snb*
Mother: *jjtj* (b)	Father: *twbj* (b)
Titles: *jrj-ꜥt wdpw*	Wife:

a. stela, Geneva, Musées d'art et d'histoire 6875, Stefanović, *SAK* 39, 2010, 313-319, Taf. 30.
b. stela, Paris, Louvre C42 (unpublished).

Literature:

Dating: 13th Dynasty

Dossier No. 130	*rn-snb*
Mother: *nbt-pr ḥnwj* (a)	Father: *zẖ3w n w nḫtj* (a)
Titles: *wꜥb n jmn*	Wife:

a. stela, London, BM EA 851, Stefanović, *Journal of Classical Studies Matica Srpska* 12, 2010, 59-62.
b. stela, London BM EA 1348, *HTBM* IV, pl. 27.

[uncertain]

Literature: Bourriau, *Pharaohs and Mortals*, no. 45

Dating: 13th / 17th Dynasty

Dossier No. 131	*rn-snb*
Mother:	Father:
Titles: *wꜥb ḥwt-ḥrw* [*nbt*] *jwnt* (a) *wꜥb ḥwt-ḥrw nbt jwnt* (b)	Wife:

a. seal, London BM EA 41564, Martin, *Seals*, 831.
b. stela, New York, MMA 69.30, Fischer, *Egyptian Studies* III, 128-129, pl. 21.

Literature: Fischer, *Egyptian Studies* III, 127.

Dating: 13th Dynasty

Dossier No. 132	*rn-snb*
Mother:	Father:
Titles: *wdpw*	Wife:

a. stela, Musées d'art et d'histoire, Genève 6875, Stefanović, *SAK* 39, 2010, 313-319, Taf. 30.
b. stela, London, BM EA 225, *HTBM* III, pl. 10.

[uncertain]

Literature:

Dating: 13th Dynasty

Dossier No. 133	*rn-snb*
Mother: *nfrt-jw* (c)	Father: *šmsw ddj* (a)
Titles: *rḫ-nswt*	Wife: *nbw-jb* (a)

a. stela, Bolton 20.10. 12, Stefanović, *SAK* 38, 2009, 297–309.
b. stela, Berlin 7311, Simpson, *ANOC* 22, pl. 32.
c. stela, Cairo, CG 20614, Lange-Schäfer, *CCG* II, 253-254.

[uncertain]

Literature:

Dating: 13th Dynasty / Neferhotep I

Dossier No. 134	*rn-snb*
Mother: *z3t-ḫnmw*	Father: *jj-ḏs.f* (b)
Titles: *ḥrj-pr n pr ꜥ3*	Wife:

a. stela, Lacock Abbey 50028, Satzinger-Stefanović, in: *From Illahun to Djeme*, 241-243.
b. stela, Marseille, Musée d'Archéologie méditerranéenne 227, Satzinger-Stefanović, *From Illahun to Djeme*, 243-244.

Literature: Satzinger-Stefanović, in: *From Illahun to Djeme*, 244-245.

Dating: 13th Dynasty

Dossier No. 135	*rn.f-snb / zj-n-wsrt*
Mother:	Father:
Titles: *jmj-r ẖnrt*	Wife:

a. seal, Martin, *Seals*, 854a.
b. seal impression, Los Angeles, Los Angeles County Museum of Art M.80.202.861.

[the same person is perhaps attested on the statue Baltimore, Walters Art Gallery 22.166: *jmj-r ẖnrt snb / zj-n-wsrt ir.n nfrt*]

Literature:

Dating: 12th / 13th Dynasty

Dossier No. 136	*rḥw-ꜥnḫ*
Mother: *nbt-pr ppw*	Father:
Titles: *jmj-r ꜥẖnwtj n kꜣp* (a) *rḫ nswt* (b-h) *ḫtmtj-bjtj, jmj-r ḫtmtjw, sḏmj šnꜥ* (h) *ḫtmtj-bjtj, jmj-r pr wr* (i)	Wife: *nbt-pr ddt-ꜥnḳt*

a. stela, Musées d'art et d'histoire, Genève 6875, Stefanović, *SAK* 39, 2010, 313-319, Taf. 30.
b. stela, Berlin 7311, Simpson, *ANOC* 22, pl. 32.
c. stela, Cairo, CG 20104, Simpson, *ANOC* 22, pl. 32.
d. stela, Cairo, CG 20147, Simpson, *ANOC* 22, pl. 32.
e. stela, Cairo, CG 20614, Lange-Schäfer, *CCG* II, 253-254.
f. stela, Vienna, KHM ÄS 140, Hein – Satzinger, *Stelen des Mitleren Reiches* I, 55-61.
g. inscription, Wadi el-Hudi no. 24, Sadek, *Wadi el-Hudi*, 51.
h. seals, UC 11504, Martin, *Seals*, 857; Martin, *Seals*, 858.
i. statuette, Grajetzki, *Two Treasurers*, 43.

Literature: Franke, *Doss.*, no. 389 (b-h); Grajetzki, *Two Treasurers*, 43.

Dating: 13th Dynasty / Neferhotep I – Sebekhotep IV

Dossier No. 137	*rḥw-snb*

Mother:	Father:
Titles: *jmj-r st* (a) *jmj-r st n ꜥt t* (b, c)	Wife: *nbt-pr jw.s-nj* ? (a)

a. stela, Vienna KHM ÄS 181, Hein – Satzinger, *Stelen des Mitleren Reiches* I, 133-136.
b. stela, Padua, Museo Civico di Padova, Dolzani, in: *Viaggatori veneti alla scoperta dell'Egitto*, 175 (1).
c. stela, Hanover, Kestner Museum 2932, Munro, *Kerstner Museum*, no. 3.

Literature: Grajetzki, *Two Treasurers*, 54.

Dating: 13th Dynasty

Dossier No. 138	*rdj-n-ptḥ*

Mother:	Father:
Titles: *wr mḏw šmꜥw*	Wife:

a. stela, Bolton 1920.10.12, Stefanović, *SAK* 38, 2009, 297-309.
b. stela, Carnarvon - Carter, *Five Years' Exploration at Thebes*, pl. 54.

[uncertain]

Literature:

Dating: 13th Dynasty

Dossier No. 139	*rdj-n-ptḥ*
Mother:	Father:
Titles: *ẖtmtj-bjtj jmj-r sẖtjw*	Wife:

a. seal, London, UC 11342, Martin, *Seals*, 897 (?).
b. seal, Wozencroft, *GM* 213, 2007, 101-104.

Literature:

Dating: 13th Dynasty

Dossier No. 140	*ḥmw-m-š3*
Mother:	Father:
Titles: *rẖ nswt*	Wife:

a. seal, London, UC 11478, Martin, *Seals*, 1101.
b. seal, Martin, *Seals*, 1102.
c. seal, Martin, *MDAIK* 33, 1979, 36.

Literature:

Dating: 13th Dynasty

Dossier No. 141 | *ḥnjj*

Mother: Father:

Titles: *jmj-r pr* (a) Wife:

jmj-r pr n [...] (b)

a. statuette, Muscarella, *Ancient Art*, no. 184.
b. stela, Cairo, CG 20483, Lange-Schäfer, *CCG* II, 79-80.

[uncertain]

Literature:

Dating: 12th / 13th Dynasty

Dossier No. 142 | *ḥrj*

Mother: Father:

Titles: *ꜣṯw n ṯt ḥḳꜣ* Wife:

a. stela, Warsaw 141281, Engelbach, *ASAE* 22, 1922, 116-117.
b. seal, Art Inst. of Chicago 94.1558; Martin, *Seals*, 1131.
c. stela, Marée, *BMSAES* 12, 2009, fig. 16.

[all objects found at Edfu]

Literature: Stefanović, *Regular Military Titles*, no. 442 (a-b); Marée, *BMSAES* 12, 2009, 58-59.

Dating: 13th Dynasty

Dossier No. 143	*ḥrj*
Mother:	Father:
Titles: *ḥ3tj-ʿ jmj-r ḥmw-nṯr*	Wife: *nfrw*

a. stela, Cairo CG 20329, Lange-Schäfer, *CCG* I, 342.
b. fragment of offering table, Warsaw 138796; Maree, *BMSAES* 12, 2009, 52-56, fig. 13.
c. Alliot, *Edfu* 1933, 30 (4).

[all objects found at Edfu]

Literature: Maree, *BMSAES* 12, 2009, 52-56

Dating: 13th Dynasty

Dossier No. 144	*ḥrj-w3h*
Mother:	Father: *jrj-ʿt n ʿḥ snfrw*
Titles: *jrj-ʿt* (a) *jmj-r st n ḫtmt* (b)	Wife:

a. stela, Zagreb 8, Monnet Saleh, *Les antiquités égyptiennes de Zagreb*, 22-23.
b. stela Roanne 163; de Meulenaere, *CdE* 60, 1985, 119-120.

[*ḥri-w3h* is called on b *ʿ3mw* 'Asiat']

Literature: Grajetzki, *Two Treasurers*, 44.

Dating: 13th Dynasty, shortly before Neferhotep I

Dossier No. 145	*ḥrw*
Mother:	Father:
Titles: *ḥ3tj-ʿ ḫtmw-nṯr*	Wife: *nfrw*

a. statue, Cairo CG 520; Borchardt, *Statuen und Statuetten*, 79.
b. stela, Petrie, *Abydos II*, XXIX.

[father of the *ḥ3tj-ʿ ḫtmw-nṯr snb-tjfj*, Franke, *Doss*. 673]

Literature: Sauneron, *BIFAO* 51, 1952, 158-159

Dating: early 13th Dynasty (?)

Dossier No. 146	*ḥrw-m-z3.f*
Mother:	Father: *jmj-r st ddt-nšmt* (b)
Titles: *jmj-r pr*	Wife:

a. papyri, Berlin P.10024A, P.10081A-C, JE 71583, Luft, *Briefe aus Ilahun*, 49, 101-109, 119.
b. Stela, Cairo CG 20052, Lange-Schäfer, *CCG* I, 62-63.

Literature: Luft, *Briefe aus Ilahun*, 67.

Dating: 12th Dynasty / Amenemhet III

Dossier No. 147	*ḥrfw*

Mother: Father:

Titles: *jmj-r ḫtmt* Wife:
jrj-pꜥt, ḥꜣtj-ꜥ, ḫtmtj-bjtj (b, c)

a. seals, Martins, *Seals*, 1142-1143.
b. weight, London UC 16366, Petrie, *Weights and Measures*, pl. VII, pl. XL; Quirke, in: *Excavating Egypt*, 116, no. 86.
c. statue, Brooklyn Museum of Art 36.617, James, *Inscriptions*, 49 (111), pl. XXXVI (uncertain, name only partly preserved).

Literature: Grajetzki, *Beamte*, 55 (II.18).

Dating: 13th Dynasty

Dossier No. 148	*ḥḏrj*

Mother: Father:

Titles: *zꜣb r nḫn* (b) Wife:

a. stela, *Small Sculpture from Ancient Egypt* 12, Jan. 1985, no. 3.
b. stela, Leiden, Rijksmuseum van Oudheden, AP.33, Boeser, *Leiden* II, 12 (46).

[uncertain]

Literature:

Dating: 13th Dynasty

Dossier No. 149	*ẖꜥ-kꜣw-rꜥ-snb*
Mother: *nbt-pr stjt-ḥtp*	Father:
Titles: *hꜣtj-ꜥ jmj-r ḥmw-nṯr* *ẖtmtj-bjtj* (c)	Wife: *snt-snb* (e)

a. chapel in Heqaib sanctuary on Elephantine, Habachi, *Heqaib*, 55-56.
b. statue, Habachi, *Heqaib*, 56, no. 28.
c. statue, Habachi, *Heqaib*, 57, no. 29.
d. seal impressions, von Pilgrim, Untersuchungen, 224, nos. 2, 3, 50, 51, 53, 54.
e. stela, Habachi, *Heqaib*, 73-74, no. 47 (just as *ẖꜥ-kꜣw*).

Indenty of a-d and e uncertain

Literature: Franke, *Heqaib*, 43-45.

Dating: early 13th Dynasty

Dossier No. 150	*ḫww-wjj*
Mother:	Father:
Titles: *ḫtmw-nṯr* (a, b) *jmj-r spꜣt* (b)	Wife:

a. inscription, *Bi'r Minayh*, no. E 016, 182.
b. inscription, Žaba, *RILN*, no. A22, 235.
c. inscription, *Bi'r Minayh*, no. G 010, 188.

Literature: *Bi'r Minayh*, 188.

Dating: probably Middle Kingdom

Dossier No. 151	*ḫmmj*
Mother:	Father:
Titles: *z3b r3 nḫn* (a) *wr mḏw šmˁw* (b, c)	Wife:

a. stela, Vienna KHM ÄS 103, Hein – Satzinger, *Stelen des Mitleren Reiches* I, 9-12.
b. seal, Khartoum, Martin, *Seals*, 1202 (found at Mirgissa).
c. papyrus, Boulaq XVIII; Scharff, *ZÄS* 57, 1922, pl. 12**, 27.3.

[uncertain]

Literature: Franke, *Heqaib*, 67.

Dating: 13th Dynasty

Dossier No. 152	*ḫmt-nw*
Mother:	Father:
Titles: *3ṯw ˁ3 n nwt*	Wife:

a. seal, Martin, *Seals*, 1204.
b. stela in a private collection, Roccati, in: *Legacy of Berlev*, 111-113.

Literature: Stefanović, *Regular Military Titles*, no. 294.

Dating: 13th Dynasty

Dossier No. 153	*ḫnsw*
Mother:	Father: *ˁnḫ n nwt ddw-sbk* (a)
Titles: *ˁnḫ n nwt*	Wife:

a. stela, Karlsruhe H 431; Gamer-Wallert – Gerishammer, *Ägyptische Kunst*, no. 8.
b. Inscription near Abd el Qadir (Lower Nubia), Hintze-Reineke, *FSN* I, 29, no. 29.

Literature: Stefanović, *Regular Military Titles*, no. 164.

Dating: 12th / 13th Dynasty

Dossier No. 154	*ḫnsw*
Mother: *ẖkrt-nswt* (c) *jdj*	Father: *ḫtmtj-bjtj jmj-r gs-pr jj-m-jˁt-jb* (c)
Titles: *jrj-pˁt ḥ3tj-ˁ ḫtmtj-bjtj jmj-r gs-pr* (a-b) *ḫtmtj-bjtj ẖrp wsḫt* (c)	Wife:

a. stela, New York MMA 21.2.69, Hayes, *Scepter of Egypt* I, 345-356, fig. 227.
b. seal, Cairo and MMA 26.7.13, Martin, *Seals*, 1217 & 1218.
c. stela, Liverpool, World Museum 16.11.06.13, Grajetzki, *Court Officials*, 93, fig. 42, Grajetzki, *Zemathor*, 8-9, pl. X.

for the father see Franke, *Doss*. 23, add to the latter dossier the seal impression von Pilgrim, *Untersuchungen*, 242, fig. 98, no. 207.

Literature: Franke, *Doss*. 464 (a-b); Grajetzki, *Court Officials*, 93-94; Franke, in: *Studies Assmann*, 109; Grajetzki, *Zemathor*, 8-9, pl. X.

Dating: 13th Dynasty / Sobekhotep II to Sobekhotep IV

Dossier No. 155	*ẖntj-ẖtjj*
Mother:	Father:
Titles: *wḥmw n ꜥrrjt*	Wife:

a. ostraca, OG 24, Mahfouz, *Afrique & Orient* 41, 2006, 33.
b. Papyrus found at Lahun, London, UC 32114C, Collier, Quirke, *Letters*, 28-29.

Literature: Mahfouz, *Afrique & Orient* 41, 2006, 32

Dating: 12th Dynasty

Dossier No. 156	*ẖntj-ẖtjj-wr*
Mother:	Father:
Titles: *wḥmw n ꜥrrjt*	Wife:

a. seal, Martin, *Seals*, 1226 (found at Lahun).
b. Papyrus found at Lahun, London, UC 32114C, Collier, Quirke, *Letters*, 28-29.

Literature:

Dating: 12th Dynasty

Dossier No. 157	*ḫntj-ḫtjj-ḥtp*
Mother:	Father: *ptḥ* (a)
Titles: *ḫrtj-nṯr*	Wife:

a. inscription, Černy, *IS* no. 24.
b. inscription, Černy, *IS* no. 90.

Literature:

Dating: 12th Dynasty / Amenemhet III

Dossier No. 158	*ḫntj-ḫtjj-ḥtp*
Mother:	Father: *ptḥ* (a)
Titles:	Wife:

a. Lisht, tomb 384, of 'treasurer' *rḥw-r-ḏr.sn*, Arnold, *Middle Kingdom Tomb Architecture*, pl. 120a
b. stela, New York, MMA 12.182.1, Hayes, *Scepter of Egypt I*, 333, fig. 221,

[for the'treasurer' *rḥw-r-ḏr.sn* compare Franke, *Doss*. No. 391]

Literature:

Dating: 12th Dynasty

Dossier No. 159	*ẖnmw-nḫt*
Mother: *nbt-pr ẖnmw-ꜥꜣ*	Father: *ẖnmw-nḫt*
Titles: *wꜥb ꜥꜣ* *zꜣ-ḥꜣtj-ꜥ* (a)	Wife:

a. coffin and burial found at Rifeh ('Tomb of Two Brothers'), Petrie, *Gizeh and Rifeh*, pl. XIIIG; David, *Two Brothers*, 78-81
b. stela, Cairo, CG 20092, Lange-Schäfer, *CCG* I, 112-113..

Literature:

Dating: second half of 12th Dynasty

Dossier No. 160	*ẖnmw-ḥtp*
Mother: *ḫtmt tꜣt*	Father: *ẖnmw-ḥtp* (II) (a)
Titles: *jrj-pꜥt ḥꜣtj-ꜥ* (b)	Wife:

a. depicted next to his mother in the tomb of Khnumhotep II at Beni Hassan (BH 3), Newberry, *Beni Hasan*, pl, XXXV.
b. tomb at Beni Hassan (BH 4), Newberry, *Beni Hasan*, 5.

Literature: Newberry, *Beni Hasan*, 44.

Dating: 12th Dynasty (Senusret II and later)

Dossier No. 161	*ḫnmw-ḥtp*
Mother: *ḫtjj* (a)	Father: *ḫnmw-ḥtp* (II) (a)
Titles: *smr* (a) *jmj-r ʿḫnwtj* (b) *jmj-r pr wr* (c) *jmj-r nwt, ṯ3tj* (and others) (c) a. tomb of his father Khnumhotep, Beni Hassan, no. 3; Newberry, *Beni Hasan I*, pl. XXVI, XXX. b. stela, Durham N. 1935, Birch, *Catalogue*, 53. c. tomb no. 2 at Dahshur, Allen, *BASOR* 352, 2008, 29-39.	Wife:
Literature: Franke, in *Middle Kingdom Studies*, 56-67.	
Dating: Senusret II-Senusret III/Amenemhat III	

Dossier No. 162	*z3-3st*
Mother: *js-n-pr.s*	Father: *z3-mrj.s*
Titles: *jmj-r ʿḫnwtj*(a) *jmj-r pr wr* (b-c) *jmj-r pr ḫtmt, jmj-r nwtṯ3tj* (d) a. stela, London, BM EA561, *HTBM* II, pl. 25 (= Simpson, *ANOC* 41, pl. 60). b. stela, Leiden, Rijksmuseum van Oudheden AP.10 (V 71), Boeser, *Leiden* II, Tf. VIII (= Simpson, *ANOC* 41, pl. 60). c. offering table, Cairo CG 23006 (= Simpson, *ANOC* 41, pl. 60). d. tomb at Dahshur, de Morgan, *Dahchour 1894-1895*, 77-85, pl. XIV; Simpson, in: *Pyramid Studies*, 57-60, pls. 14-15; El-Husseiny - Khafagy, *EA* 36, 2010, 21-24.	Wife:
Literature: Franke, *Doss.*, no. 511 (a-c); Grajetzki, *Beamte*, 50-51 (II.9)	
Dating: 12th Dynasty / about Amenemhat II	

Dossier No. 163	*z3-j^cḥ*
Mother:	Father:
Titles: *jrj pḏt*	Wife:

a. seal, Martin, *Seals*, 1267.
b. inscription (Askut), Gratien, *Prosopographie*, 143.

Literature: Gratien, *Prosopographie*, 143; Stefanović, *Regular Military Titles*, no. 939.

Dating: late 12th/13th Dynasty

Dossier No. 164	*z3-jʿḥ*
Mother: *ḥtp*	Father: *wr-b3w.s*
Titles: *ṯ3w ʿ n zẖ3w n jmj-r ẖtmt*	Wife: *hnjjt*

a. rock inscription at Kumma, Hintze-Reineke, *FSN* I, 125, no. 447.
b. rock inscription at Kumma, Hintze-Reineke, *FSN* I, 134, no. 474.

Literature:

Dating: late 12th/13th Dynasty

Dossier No. 165	*z3-jmn*
Mother: *z3t-š3bt*	Father: *jt nṯr jnj-ḥrt jj-m-jꜥt-jb*
Titles: *jrj-pꜥt, ḥ3tj-ꜥ, ḫtmtj-bjtj,* *zḫ3w ꜥ n nswt n ḫft ḥr*	Wife:

a. stela, Burnley, Towneley Hall Art Gallery and Museums, Eg. 100, Leahy, *GM* 44, 1981, 23-28.
b. block, London, UC 16810 (title not fully preserved).

[uncertain]

Literature:

Dating: 13th / 17th Dynasty

Dossier No. 166	*z3-jmn*
Mother:	Father:
Titles: *jrj pḏt*	Wife:

a. seal, Khatoum, Martin, *Seals*, 1275 (found at Mirgissa).
b. seal, Gratien, in: *Nubische Studien*, 89-90.

Literature: Gratien, *Prosopographie*, 143; Stefanović, *Regular Military Titles*, no. 940.

Dating: 13th Dynasty

Dossier No. 167	*z3-jmn*
Mother:	Father:
Titles: *wr mdw šmꜥw*	Wife: *nbt-pr ib-iꜥw*

a. stela, Cairo CG 20188, Lange-Schäfer, *CCG* I, 158-159.
b. canopic jars of his son *snb-ḥnꜥ.f*: (Abydos, tomb D 25), Oxford, Ashmolean Musem E354; London BM EA 32709, Grajetzki, *SAK* 34, 2006, 214; Grajetzki, *Zemathor*, 41, n. 149.

[identification uncertain; common name and common title]

Literature:

Dating: 13th / 17th Dynasty

Dossier No. 168	*z3-jmn*
Mother:	Father:
Titles: *šmsw*	Wife:

a. stela, Copenhagen, Ny Carlsberg Glyptotek, ÆIN 964; Koefoed-Petersen, *Stele eg. Kopenhague*, no. 16; Jørgensen, *Catalogue Egypt I (3000-15500 B.C.)*, 190-191, no. 79.
b. stela, New York, MMA 68.14; Fischer, *Egyptian Studies* III, 129-130, pl. 25.

Literature: Stefanović, *Regular Military Titles*, no. 691.

Dating: 13th Dynasty / Sebekhotep II

Dossier No. 169	*z3-nbt-jwnt*

Mother: *nbt-pr rs* Father: *šmsw z3-sbk*

Titles: *ꜥnḫ n ṯt ḥḳ3* Wife:

a. stela, Paris, Louvre C 145, Pierret, *Inscr. du Louvre* II, 49.
b. stela, Paris, Louvre C 253.

Literature: See: Stefanović, *Regular Military Titles*, no. 371.

Dating: Late 12th / 13th Dynasty

Dossier No. 170	*z3-nfrt*

Mother: *z3t-rꜥ* Father:

Titles: *jmj-r pr wr* Wife:
jmj-r šnwty (b)
jrj-pꜥt, ḥ3tj-ꜥ, ḫtmtj-bjtj,
smr-wꜥtj (b)
jmj-r pr (c)

a. stela, Leiden, Rijksmuseum van Oudheden AP. 30, Boeser, *Leiden* II, pl. 29.
b. statue, Habachi, *Heqaib*, no. 67.
c. fragment of the offering table, Arnold, *Pyramid of Senwosret* I, 97, fig. 43 (uncertain).

Literature: Franke, *Heqaib*, 56-58; Grajetzki, *Beamte*, 85 (III.9); Arnold, *GM* 122, 1991, 13.

Dating: 12th Dynasty / Senusret I – Amenemhat II

Dossier No. 171	*z3-ptḥ*
Mother:	Father:
Titles: *jmj-r gnwtjw*	Wife:

a. seal, Martin, *Seals*, 1287- 1288.
b. seal, Giveon, *CdE* 98, 1974, 231 (4), fig. 3.

Literature:

Dating: 13th / 17th Dynasty

Dossier No. 172	*z3-ptḥ*
Mother:	Father:
Titles: *sšrjj nswt*	Wife:

a. seal, Cairo, JE 75142, Martin, *Seals*, 1293.
b. seal, Giveon, *CdE* 98, 1974, 231 (2).

Literature:

Dating: 13th / 17th Dynasty

Dossier No. 173	*z3-nmtj*
Mother:	Father:
Titles: *šmsw*	Wife:

a. seal, Martin, *Seals*, 1306 (found at the Fort of Serra East).
a. seal, Patch, *Reflections of Greatness*, 61 no. 12.

Literature: Stefanović, *Regular Military Titles*, no. 694 (a).

Dating: 13th Dynasty

Dossier No. 174	*z3-ḥwt-ḥr / bsj/bjs*
Mother: *nbt-pr snb-dd.tw* (b)	Father:
Titles: *hrj-ḥbt n pr-nfr* (a) *ẖrj-ḥbt* (b)	Wife:

a. stela, London, BM EA 833 + Laval, Museé du Vieux Château, 4560, Clère, *JEA* 68, 1982, 69-75, pl. 6.
b. stela, Cairo, JE 39754, Mareé, in: *The Second Intermediate Period*, 245 (k), pl. 63.

[The same person is, perhaps, attested on stela Liverpool, Garstang Museum E.77. See Mareé, in: *The Second Intermediate Period*, 270]

Literature: Mareé, in: *The Second Intermediate Period*, 269-270.

Dating: 13th Dynasty

Dossier No. 175	*z3-sbk*
Mother: *jmnjj* (c)	Father: *ˁnḫ n nwt rsw* (c)
Titles: *smsw h3jjt*	Wife: *jtj* (c)

a. seal, Martin, *Seals,* 1337.
b. seal, Martin, *MDAIK* 33, 1979, 217.
c. stela, Liverpool, World Museum M13927.

Literature:

Dating: 12th / 13th Dynasty

Dossier No. 176	*z3-sbk*
Mother:	Father:
Titles: *zẖ3w ḳdwt*	Wife:

a. stela, London, BM EA 215, *HTBM* III, pl. 46 (= Simpson, *ANOC* 21,5)
b. stela, Cairo, CG 20479, Lange-Schäfer, *CCG* I, 356-357.

[Stela (a) belongs to the 'treasurer' *snb-sw-m-ˁ(.j)*, Grajetzki, *Two Treasurers*, 21]

Literature: Grajetzki, *Two Treasurers*, 44

Dating: 13th Dynasty / about Sobekhotep II – Neferhotep I (a)

Dossier No. 177	*z3-sbk*
Mother: *nbt-pr nj-sw*	Father:
Titles: *šmsw*	Wife: *nbt-pr rs*

a. stela, Paris, Louvre C 145, Pierret, *Inscr. du Louvre* II, 49.
b. stela, Paris, Louvre C 253.

Literature: See: Franke, *Doss.*, 546; Stefanović, *Regular Military Titles*, no. 699.

Dating: Late 12th / 13th Dynasty

Dossier No. 178	*z3-sbk*
Mother:	Father:
Titles: *smsw h3jjt*	Wife:

a. seal, Martin, *Seals*, 1337.
b. seal, Martin, *MDAIK* 33, 1979, 27.

Literature:

Dating: 13th Dynasty

Dossier No. 179	*zj-n-wsrt*	
Mother: *nbt-pr kstj* ? (a)		Father:
Titles: *jmj-r pr*		Wife:

a. stela, Cambridge, Fitzwilliam Museum E.60.1926, Martin, *Stelae*, no. 22.
b. seal, London, BM EA 41568, Martin, *Seals*, 1244.
c. seal, Wegner, *JARCE* 35, 1998, 34-37 (18).

[uncertain]

Literature:

Dating: late 12th / 13th Dynasty

Dossier No. 180	*zšn / zꜣ-ḥwt-ḥr*	
Mother: *tjtj*		Father:
Titles: *ḫrp srḳt*		Wife:

a. statue, Munich, StaatlicheSammlung Ägyptischer Kunst, ÄS 5361 + 7211, Grimm, *Zeitschrift für Wissenschaft und Kunst in Bayern* 3, 2002, 44-46; Fischer-Elfert - Grimm, *ZÄS* 130, 2003, 60-80.
b. statue, Schildkraut - Solia, *Egypt at the Merrin Gallery*, no. 9.

Literature:

Dating: 12th Dynasty / Sesostris II

Dossier No. 181	*sʿnḫ*
Mother: *nfrt*	Father: *zj-nj-wst* (b)
Titles: *jmj-r mrt*	Wife:

a. stela, Cambridge, Fitzwilliam, E. 207.1900; Martin, *Stelae*, 23-25, no. 17.
b. stela, Cambridge, Fitzwilliam, E.273.1900; Martin, *Stelae*, 32-33, no. 20.

Literature:

Dating: end of 12th Dynasty

Dossier No. 182	*sʿnḫ-ḥrw*
Mother: *sbk-ḥtp* (a)	Father:
Titles:	Wife: *z3t-mnṯw* (a) *nḫt-nfrt* (b)

a. stela, Paris, Louvre C181, Gayet, *Stèles de la XIIe dynastie*, 10, 6, pl. 35.
b. stela, Paris, Louvre C245.

Literature: Freed, in: *Studies Simpson* I, 327-329, 331-334.

Dating: 12th Dynasty / Senwosret I – Amenemhet II

Dossier No. 183	*sbk-ꜥꜣ*
Mother: *jꜣjjt* (a)	Father:
Titles: *ꜥnḫ n nwt*	Wife:

a. inscription, Gasse-Randot, *Séhel*, SEH 198.
b. inscription, Gasse-Randot, *Séhel*, SEH 199.

Literature:

Dating: 13th Dynasty

Dossier No. 184	*sbk-ꜥꜣ bbi*
Mother:	Father:
Titles: *ḫtmtj-bjtj jmj-r ḫnrt* (a, b) *jmj-r nwt ṯꜣtj* (b)	Wife:

a. seal, Martin, BM EA 32295, *Seals*, no. 1385.
b. seal, Martin, *Seals*, nos. 448-449 (ony as *bbi*).
c. seals, Cairo JE 63905 (found at Lisht), Martin, *Seals*, 1383 and 1384.

Literature: Vernus, *Surnom* , 57, no. 263; Ryhold, *Second Intermediate Period*, 260; Grajetzki, *Beamte*, 23 (I.22).

Dating: 13th Dynasty

Dossier No. 185	*sbk-n.j-pw*

Mother:	Father:
Titles: *wdpw* (b-c) *jmj-r st n ꜥt jwf* (d)	Wife:

a. stela, Musées d'art et d'histoire, Genève 6875, Stefanović, *SAK* 39, 2010, 313-319, Taf. 30.
b. stela, London, BM EA 238, *HTMB* III, pl. 15 (= Simpson, *ANOC* 54, pl. 76).
c. stela, New York, Brooklyn 37.1349E, James, *Brooklyn Museum* I, no. 104c, pl. LXXXVIII.
d. stela, Dublin UC 1360, Quirke, *RdÉ* 51, 2000, 225-230.

Literature: Franke, *Doss.,* no. 564 (b-c); Grajetzki, *Two Treasurers*, 23-24.

Dating: 13th Dynasty

Dossier No. 186	*sbk-nḫt*

Mother:	Father:
Titles: *ḫtmtj-bjtj, jmj-r mšꜥ*	Wife:

a. seal, New York, MMA 30.8.669, Martin, *Seals*, 1412.
b. seal, Jerusalem, Israel Museum 76.31.4595, Ben-Tor, *Scarab*, no. 3.

Literature: Grajetzki, *Beamte*, 111, no. IV.27; Stefanović, *Regular Military Titles*, no. 1045.

Dating: 13th Dynasty

Dossier No. 187	*sbk-ḥtp*
Mother:	Father: *ꜣṯw n ṯt ḥkꜣ jꜥtw* (a)
Titles: *jmj-ḫt zꜣ pr*	Wife:

a. stela, Cambridge, Fitzwilliam; E.SS.45; Martin, *Stelae*, 50-51, no. 30.
b. stela, Regen – Soukiassian, *Gebel El-Zeit* II, no. 25 (SA 800).

Literature: Marée, *BiOr* 66, 2009, 162

Dating: 13th Dynasty

Dossier No. 188	*sbk-ḥtp*
Mother: *nbt-pr mrw* (b)	Father:
Titles: *jmj-r pr*	Wife: *nbt-pr tjtw* (a)

a. stela, St. Petersburg, 1084; Bolshakov - Quirke, *Middle Kingdom Stelae*, 53-57, pl. 11.
b. statue, Wild, *BIFAO* 69, 1970, 90-97 (from the Fayum?).

Literature: Verbovsek, *Private Tempelstatuen*, 458-459.

Dating: 13th Dynasty, Sobekhotep II – Neferhotep I

Dossier No. 189	*sbk-ḥtp*

Mother:	Father:
Titles: *wr mḏw šmꜥw*	Wife: *bꜣkt nt ḥḳꜣ ddi* (a)

a. stela, Glasgow AGM 1923.33 ac, Grajetzki, *GM* 224, 2010, 47-58.
b. stela, London BM EA 245, *HTBM* IV, pl. 45.

[uncertain]

Literature: Mareé, in: *The Second Intermediate Period*, 244-245, 274.

Dating: 13th Dynasty

Dossier No. 190	*sbk-ḥtp*

Mother: *zꜣt-jmn*	Father:
Titles: *zꜣb r nḫn*	Wife:

a. statue, Paris, Louvre N.1587, Delange, *Catalogue des statues égyptiennes*, 100-101.
b. stela, Chicago OIM, 7779, Petrie - Weigall, *Abydos* I, pl. 60/4.

Literature:

Dating: 13th Dynasty

Dossier No. 191	*sbk-ḥtp ḥꜥkw*
Mother: *nt-nbw*	Father: *wꜥb rs-snb*
Titles: *wr ḫrp ḥmmwt*	Wife:

a. seal, Martin, *Seals*, no. 1149.
b. statue, Schulman, in: *Mempihs et ses necropolis au Nouvel Empire*, pl. 11 .

Literature: Grajetzki, *Beamte*, 111.

Dating: 13th Dynasty

Dossier No. 192	*snꜥꜥ-jb*
Mother:	Father:
Titles: *smsw hꜣjjt*	Wife:

a. seal, London, BM EA 4316, Martin, *Seals*, 1479.
b. seal, Giveon, *GM* 67, 1983, 34.

Literature: Giveon, *GM* 67, 1983, 36 (6)

Dating: 13th / 17th Dynasty

Dossier No. 193	*sn(j)-ʿnḫ*
Mother:	Father: *wr-b3w-ptḥ*
Titles: *jmj-r pr wr* (a) *jmj-r ḫtmtjw* (b)	Wife:
a. stela, Cairo, CG 20284, Lange-Schäfer, *CCG* I, 300-301. b. statue, Vienna, KHM ÄS 61, Jaroš-Deckert, *Statuen* I, 14-17.	
Literature: Grajetzki, *Beamte*, 104 (III.58)	
Dating: 12th /13th Dynasty	

Dossier No. 194	*snfrw*
Mother: *nbt-pr rsst*	Father:
Titles: *jrj-ʿt n ʿḥ*	Wife:
a. stela, Zagreb 8, Monnet Saleh, *Les antiquités égyptiennes de Zagreb*, 22-23. b. statue, Habachi, *Heqaib*, 93, no. 69.	
Literature: Franke, *Heqaib*, 65-66.	
Dating: 13th Dynasty / shortly before Neferhotep I	

Dossier No. 195	*snfrw*
Mother:	Father:
Titles: *ḥ3tj-ʿ, jmj-r ḥwt-nṯr*	Wife:

a. seal, Cairo, JE 75077, Martin, *Seals*, 1617.
b. inscription, Petrie, *Season*, pl. VIII, no. 182.

Literature:

Dating: 13th Dynasty

Dossier No. 196	*snb*
Mother: *jjj*	Father: *ẖtjj* (a)
Titles:	Wife:

a. stela, Vienna KHM ÄS 136, Hein – Satzinger, *Stelen des Mitleren Reiches* I, 28-32.
b. statuette, Vercoutter, *Mirgissa* II, 136, fig. 49/8.

Literature:

Dating: 12th /13th Dynasty

Dossier No. 197	*snb*
Mother: *snb.tjsj* (a)	Father:
Titles: *jmj-r w* (a) *jmj-r w n šnʿ* (b)	Wife:

a. stela, Cairo CG 20051, Lange-Schäfer, *CCG* I, 60-62.
b. stela, Vienna KHM ÄS 132, Hein – Satzinger, *Stelen des Mitleren Reiches* I, 34-38.

Literature: Russo, *Territory w*, 31-32, 54, pl. III.

Dating: 12th /13th Dynasty

Dossier No. 198	*snb*
Mother: *ddt-sbk* (a, d, e)	Father:
Titles: *jmj-r st n ʿt ḥnḳt* (a) *wdpw n ʿt ḥnḳt* (b) *jmj-r ʿẖnwtj n k3p* (c-g)	Wife:

a. stela, Musées d'art et d'histoire, Genève 6875, Stefanović, *SAK* 39, 2010, 313-319, pl. 30/
b. stela, Cairo CG 20266, Lange-Schäfer, *CCG* I, 284-285.
c. stela, Berlin 7311, Simpson, *ANOC* 22, pl. 32/
d. stela Cairo, CG 20614, Lange-Schäfer, *CCG* II, 253-254.
e. stela, Vienna, KHM ÄS 140, Hein – Satzinger, *Stelen des Mitleren Reiches* I, 55-61.
f. inscription, Wadi el-Hudi no. 24, Sadek, *Wadi el-Hudi*, 51.
g. seal, Aswan, Martin, *Seals*, 1480 (found at Quban, Cemetery 110, tomb 267).

Literature: Franke, *Doss.*, no. 628 (c-g); Grajetzki, *Two Treasurers*, 44.

Dating: 13th Dynasty / Neferhotep I – Sebekhotep IV

Dossier No. 199	*snbj*
Mother: *jnj-jtj.f-ꜥnḫ* (? c)	Father: *ẖnmw-ḥtp* (c)
Titles: *jmj-r pr* (a, b, c) *jmj-r ẖwjjt* (a, c)	Wife:

a. coffin found at Meir, Kamal, *ASAE* 11, 1911, 28-29/
b. canopic box, New York MMA 11.150.17A 1-3; Kamal, *ASAE* 11, 1911, 30-31; Lüscher, *Kanopenkästen* 106, no. 63/
c. stela, Kamal, *ASAE* 12, 1912, 97-98/

all objects are most likely from his burial at Meir

Literature: Willems, *Chests of Life*, 89, 97.

Dating: 12th Dynasty, Senusret I or shortly after

Dossier No. 200	*snbj*
Mother: *jww* (a)	Father:
Titles: *ẖtmtj-bjtj jmj-r ẖtmt*	Wife:

a. statue, Sotheby's 1988, no. 85.
b. seal, Martin, *Seals* 1499.

Literature: Franke, Heqaib, 67, Grajetzki, Beamte, 159 (VIII.2).

Dating: 13th Dynasty

Dossier No. 201	*snbj-šrj*
Mother: *jww* (a)	Father:
Titles: *rḫ nswt* (a) *jmj-r pr wr*	Wife:

a. stela, Vienna KHM ÄS 168; Hein - Satzinger, *Stelen des Mitleren Reiches* I, 113-115.
b. offering table, Marseille 252; *Portes pour l'au-delà l'Egypte, le Nil* et le *"Champ des offrandes"*, 147, 192, no. 37.
c. stela, St. Petersburg, 1084; Bolshakov - Quirke, *Middle Kingdom Stelae*, 53-57, pl. 11.

[Appears on c together with the 'treasurer' *snb-sw-m-ʿ(.j)*, Grajetzki, *Two Treasurers*, 21]

Literature: Bolshakov-Quirke, *Hermitage*, 56 (k); Grajetzki, *Beamte*, 92, III.24.

Dating: 13th Dynasty, Sobekhotep III – Neferhotep I (c)

Dossier No. 202	*snbw*
Mother:	Father:
Titles: *z3b r nḫn*	Wife:

a. stela, Turin, Museo Egizio Suppl. 18124.
b. stela, Tübinen, Ägyptologisches Institut der Universität Tübinen 462, Brunner-Traut – Brunner, *Sammlung der Universität Tübinen*, 84-85, Taf. 54 (Simpson, *ANOC* 60, pl. 42).

Literature:

Dating: 13th Dynasty

Dossier No. 203	*snb.f*
Mother:	Father:
Titles: *ꜣṯw n ṯt ḥḳꜣ*	Wife:

a. stela, Alnwick Castle Collection no. 1947; Birch, *Catalogue*, 290.
b. seal, Martin, *MDAIK* 35, 1979, 220, no. 29.

Literature: Stefanović, *Regular Military Titles*, no. 468.

Dating: 13th Dynasty

Dossier No. 204	*snb.f*
Mother:	Father:
Titles: *jmj-r pr wr* *ẖtmtj-bjtj* (b)	Wife:

a. stela, Pirelli, *RdE* 58, 2007, 89-90, pl. XVII.
b. papyrus, London BM EA10371 + 10435, Pirelli, *RdE* 58, 2007, 92-93.

Literature: Pirelli, *RdE* 58, 2007, 89-90

Dating: 12th Dynasty / Amenemhat III (a)

Dossier No. 205	*snb.f*

Mother: *jkj*	Father:
Titles: *jmj-r ḫtmt* *ḫtmtj-bjtj smr-wꜥtj* *jrj-pꜥt, ḥ3tj-ꜥ* (a)	Wife:

a. stela, Florence 2500, Bosticco, *Stele*, 33-35, no. 30.
b. seal, UC 11503, Martin, *seals*, no. 1606.

Literature: Grajetzki, *Beamte*, 53, no. II.13.

Dating: 13th Dynasty

Dossier No. 206	*snb.f*

Mother: *wꜥbt n ḫnsw smnt* (a)	Father: *zẖ3w n w rs-snb* (a)
Titles: *smsw h3jjt*	Wife:

a. stela, Cairo CG 20056, Lange-Schäfer, *CCG* I, 66-68.
b. stela, Vienna KHM ÄS 92, Hein – Satzinger, *Stelen des Mitleren Reiches* II, 17-19.

[uncertain]

Literature:

Dating: 13th Dynasty

Dossier No. 207	*snb.f-n.j*
Mother:	Father: *smsw h3jjt snb-sn* (a)
Titles: *smsw h3jjt*	Wife: *nbt-pr jb-jꜥw* (a)

a. stela, Marseille, Musée Borely no. 24, Maspero, *RT* 13, 1890, 114-116.
b. seal, New York, MMA 26.7.306, Martin, *Seals*, 1577.

[uncertain]

Literature:

Dating: 13th Dynasty

Dossier No. 208	*snbbw*
Mother: *z3t-nfrt-tm*	Father: *mšꜥ ḥḳ3-jb*
Titles: *jmj-r mšꜥ* (a) *jrj-pꜥt, ḥ3tj-ꜥ, ḫtmtj-bjtj,* *smr-wꜥtj* (b)	Wife:

a. stela and naos, Leiden, Rijksmuseum van Oudheden AP.80 (V 119/120), Boeser, *Leiden* II, Tf. VIII (= Simpson, *ANOC* 35.1).
b. statue, Habachi, *Heqaib*, 75-76, no. 49.

Literature: Grajetzki, *Beamte*, 119, IV.6; Franke, *Heqaib*, 51-55; Stefanović, *Regular Military Titles*, 1054.

Dating: 12th Dynasty / Senusert I – Amenemhat II

Dossier No. 209	*snb-mj-jw*
Mother: *nbt-pr ḥpjw* (a)	Father:
Titles: *jmj z3w pr*	Wife:

a. ushabti, Cairo CG 48482.
c. stela, Vienna KHM ÄS 166, Hein – Satzinger, *Stelen des Mitleren Reiches* I, 103-106.

Literature:

Dating: 13th / 17th Dynasty

Dossier No. 210	*snb-mj-jw*
Mother:	Father: *ḥry ḫ3wt mntw-ḥtp* (?)
Titles: *wr mḏw šmʿw*	Wife:

a. stela, Turin, Museo Egizio Cat. 1582.
b. papyrus, Boulaq XVIII; Scharff, *ZÄS* 57, 1922, pl. 23**, 45.12.

Literature:

Dating: 13th Dynasty / Sebekhotep II

Dossier No. 211	*snb-r-ꜣw*
Mother:	Father:
Titles: *wr mḏw šmꜥw*	Wife: */// bꜣkt nt ḥḳꜣ*

a. stela, Odessa AM, s.n., Mareé, in: *The Second Intermediate Period*, 244 (g), pl. 59.
b. pseudonaos, Vernus, *RdE* 26, 1974, 100-114.

[uncertain]

Literature: Mareé, in: *The Second Intermediate Period*, 273-274.

Dating: 13th Dynasty

Dossier No. 212	*snb.tjfj*
Mother: *kmt* (a)	Father:
Titles: *zẖꜣw ꜥ n niswt n ḫft-ḥr* *ẖtmtj-bjtj*	Wife:

a. stela, Vienna KHM ÄS 136, Hein – Satzinger, *Stelen des Mitleren Reiches* I, 48-42.
b. statue, London BM EA 24385, Grajetzki, *Beamte*, 173, X.11, b.

Literature: Grajetzki, *Beamte*, 172-73, X.11

Dating: 13th Dynasty

Dossier No. 213	*sn-pw*
Mother:	Father:
Titles: *ṯ3w n ḫft-ḥr*	Wife:

a. seal, London, BM EA 32270, Martin, *Seals*, 1465.
b. seal, Martin, *MDAIK* 33, 1979, 224 (49).

Literature:

Dating: 13th / 17th Dynasty

Dossier No. 214	*snn(j)*
Mother: *nbt-pr ttj*	Father: *km-n.j*
Titles: *rḫ nswt*	Wife:

a. stela, Cairo, CG 20282, Lange-Schäfer, *CCG* I, 297-298 (= Affara, *GM* 200, 2004, 13-26).
b. stela, Cairo, CG 20614, Lange-Schäfer, *CCG* II, 253-254.
c. stela, St. Petersburg, Hermitage 1084, Bolshakov-Quirke, *Hermitage*, 53-57.
d. stela, Vienna, KHM ÄS 200, Hein – Satzinger, *Stelen des Mitleren Reiches* II, 136-139
e. statue, Habachi, *Heqaib*, 89-90, no. 63.
f. stela, Liverpool, World Museum M13661, Grajetzki, *Two Treasurers*, pl. I.

Literature: Franke, *Doss.,* 682 (a-c); Grajetzki, *Two Treasurers*, 45

Dating: 13th Dynasty / Neferhotep I - Sebekhotep IV

Dossier No. 215	*sḥtp-jb-rʿ*
Mother: *ḥrw-mrt* (a)	Father:
Titles: *ʿnḫ n nwt*	Wife: *ḥrw-m-rʿw* (a)

a. inscription at Abu Sir (Lower Nubia), Hintze-Reineke, *FSN* I, 44, no. 95a-b, pl. 42.
b. inscription, Petrie, *Season*, pl. VII, no. 152.

Literature: Stefanović, *Regular Military Titles*, no. 231.

Dating: 12th / 13th Dynasty

Dossier No. 216	*skt*
Mother:	Father:
Titles: *z3-nswt*	Wife:

a. seals, Martin, *Seals*, 1656-1661.
b. seal, Martin, *MDAIK* 33, 1979, 226 (83).

Literature:

Dating: 13th Dynasty

Dossier No. 217	*šbnw*
Mother: *bwtw*	Father: *nmtj-nḫt*
Titles: *jmj-r ʿẖnwtj n pr ḥḏ* *jmj-r ʿẖnwtj ẖrp k3wt*	Wife:

a. statue, Habachi, *Heqaib*, 93-94, no. 70.
b. Graffiti on blocks of Khendjer pyramid, Arnold, *Control Notes*, 176-177 (Kh 1, Kh 7).
c. inscription, Petrie, *Season*, pl. I, no. 22.

Literature: Franke, *Heqaib*, 66

Dating: 13th Dynasty / Khendjer (b)

Dossier No. 218	*sḏd-ḥr*
Mother:	Father:
Titles: *šmsw*	Wife:

a. inscription, Gasse-Randot, *Séhel*, SEH 189.
b. inscription, Gasse-Randot, *Séhel*, SEH 190.

Literature:

Dating: 12th / 13th Dynasty

Dossier No. 219	*šmsw.j*

Mother: *k3jjt* (a) Father:

Titles: *šmsw nb t3wj* (b) Wife:

a. offering table Berlin 30/66; Kamal, *ASAE* 16, 1916, 96; Kaiser, Berlin, 42-43, no. 429.
b. stela, Ann Arbor, Kelsey Museum of Archaeology 1971.02.0190.

[uncertain]

Literature:

Dating: 13th / 17th Dynasty

Dossier No. 220	*ḳwpnn*

Mother: Father:

Titles: *z3-nswt smsw* Wife:

a. seal, Martin, *Seals*, 1679.
b. seal, BM EA 65963, Martin, *Seals*, 1680.
c. seal, UC 11599-11600, Martin, *Seals*, 1681-1682.
d. seal, Cairo JE 74966, Martin, *Seals*, 1683.
e. seal, Louvre, Martin, *Seals*, 1684.
f. seal, Martin, *MDAIK* 33, 1979, 224 (79).

Literature: Miniaci, in: *Il tempio e il suo personale nell'antico Egitto*, 125 (48).

Dating: 13th / 17th Dynasties

Dossier No. 221	*k3pw*
Mother:	Father:
Titles: *jrj-ˁt* (b)	Wife:

a. stela, Aswan Museum no. 1482, Sadek, *Wadi el-Hudi* I, no. 20 (11).
b. seal, Martin, *MDAIK* 35, 1979, 218 (22).

[uncertain]

Literature:

Dating: 12th Dynasty / Amenemhat III

Dossier No. 222	*kwtw*
Mother: *ḫntjj-ẖtjj* (a) / *z3t-ḫntjj-ẖtjj* (b)	Father:
Titles: *jmj-r šnˁwtj* (a) *jmj-r ˁẖnwtj* (b)	Wife: *jtj*

a. stela, Pittsburgh, The Carnegie Museum of Natural History 21538-38, Patch, *Reflections of Greatness*, no. 18.
b. stela, Cairo CG 20075, Lange-Schäfer, *CCG* I, 89-92 (= ANOC 17.1, pl. 26).

Literature:

Dating: 13th Dynasty

Dossier No. 223	*kmz*

Mother: *nbt-pr nfrt-jw*	Father:
Titles: *jmj ḫt nfw* (a) *ꜥnḫ n nwt* (b) *wdpw nfw* (c)	Wife: *jn.ṯn-sj*

a. stela, Vienna, KHM ÄS 105, Hein – Satzinger, *Stelen des Mitleren Reiches,* I 18-22.
b. stela, Vienna, KHM ÄS 156; Hein –Satzinger, *Stelen des Mitleren Reiches* I, 84-91.
c. stela, Vienna, KHM ÄS 136; Hein –Satzinger, *Stelen des Mitleren Reiches* I, 48-54.

Literature: Franke, *Doss.,* 722 (a-b); Hein –Satzinger, *Stelen des Mitleren Reiches* I, 18-19.

Dating: 13th Dynasty

Dossier No. 224	*kkw*

Mother: *jb*	Father:
Titles: *jmj-r pr*	Wife:

a. stela, London, BM EA 129, *HTBM* II, pl. 42.
b. stela, London, BM EA 131, *HTBM* I, pl. 56.

Literature:

Dating: 12th Dynasty

Dossier No. 225	*gbw / gbw-wr*
Mother: *tjtj* (b)	Father:
Titles: *wdpw* (a) *wdpw n ˁt ḥnḳt* (b) *jmj-r st n ˁt ḥnḳt* (c) a. stela, London BM EA 249, *HTBM* III, pl. 20 (= Simpson, *ANOC* 50.4, pl. 68). b. stela, Turin 1613, Maspero, *RT* 3, 1882, 122 (XV). c. seal, London, UC 11341A, Martin, *Seals*, 1349.	Wife:
Literature:	
Dating: late 12th Dynasty	

Dossier No. 226	*gnm(w)*
Mother: *nbt-pr snb-dd.tw*	Father:
Titles: *rḫtj* (a, c) a. stela, Cairo, JE 39754, Mareé, in: *The Second Intermediate Period*, 245 (k), pl. 63. b. stela, Cairo, CG 20307, Lange-Schäfer, *CCG* I, 319. c. stela, Liverpool, Garstang Museum, E.77, Amer, *GM* 171, 1999, 19-23.	Wife:
Literature: Mareé, in: *The Second Intermediate Period*, 269-270.	
Dating: 13th Dynasty	

Dossier No. 227	*ttj*
Mother: *ktms*	Father:
Titles: *jmj-r ꜥẖnwtj* (a) *jmj-r ꜥẖnwtj wr n pr-ḥḏ* (b-c)	Wife:

a. seal, Berlin 3622, Martin, *Seals*, 1728.
b. inscriptions, Petrie, *Season*, pl. I, nos. 29, 20, 46, pl. IV, no. 94, pl. V, nos. 112, 127, pl. VI, nos. 140+147+148.
c. inscription, *DeM*, 74, no. 52.

Literature: Franke, *Doss.,* 737 (b-c).

Dating: 13th Dynasty

Dossier No. 228	*ttj*
Mother:	Father:
Titles: … *ṯt-ḥkꜣ* (a) *ꜣṯw n ṯt-ḥkꜣ* (b)	Wife:

a. model coffin, BM EA 35016; Grajetzki, *BMSAES* 5, 2006, 1-12.
b. rishi coffin, Cairo, TR 19.11.27.5, Miniaci, *Rishi Coffins*, 230-231.

[uncertain: common name and common title]

Literature: Miniaci, *Rishi Coffins*, 129, n. 911

Dating: 13th Dynasty

Dossier No. 229	*ṯ3w-m-ʿntjw*
Mother:	Father:
Titles: *ḥrj-pr* (a) *sfṯ* (b) a. stela, Cairo, CG 20018, Lange-Schäfer, *CCG* I, 17-18. b. stela, St. Petersburg, Hermitage 1064, Bolshakov-Quirke, *Hermitage*, no. 22.	Wife:
Literature: Bolshakov-Quirke, *Hermitage*, 102 (m).	
Dating: 13th Dynasty / Sebekhotep II - Khendjer	

Dossier No. 230	*ṯnw*
Mother:	Father:
Titles: *jdnw n jmj-r ḫtmt* a. seal, Cairo, JE 75043, Martin, *Seals*, 1741. b. seal, Martin, *MDAIK* 35, 1979, 218 (19).	Wife:
Literature: late 12th / 13th Dynasty	
Dating:	

Dossier No. 231	*dd.tw*
Mother:	Father:
Titles: *rḫ nswt*	Wife:

a. seal, BM EA 4322, Martin, *Seals*, 1759.
b. seal, BM EA 30523, Martin, *Seals*, 1760.
c. seal, MMA 22.1.317, Martin, *Seals*, 1761 (found at Lisht).
d. seal, Cairo JE 75056, Martin, *Seals*, 1762.
e. seal, Louvre, Martin, *Seals*, 1763.
f. seal, Louvre, Martin, *Seals*, 1764-1765.
g. heart scarab, Leiden, Rijksmuseum van Oudheden, L.II.6, Quirke, *JEOL* 37, 2003, 32.

Literature:

Dating: 13th Dynasty

Dossier No. 232	*ddw-sbk*
Mother: *snt*	Father: *ḥbj* (b)
Titles: *jmj-r ˁẖnwtj*	Wife:

a. stela, Oxford, Ashmolean Museum 1954.25, Freed, in: *Studies Simpson* I, 303-307, fig. 2 (c).
b. stela, formerly in Liverpool Museum M13865, Gatty, *Mayer Collection* I, no. 144.

[uncertain]

Literature:

Dating: late 11th / early 12th Dynasty

Dossier No. 233	*ddw-sbk / rn.f-snb*
Mother: *ʿnḫ-n-jt* (e)	Father:
Titles: *rḫ nswt, ḫrp ʿḥ*	Wife:

a. inscription, Černy, *IS*, no. 51.
b. inscription, Černy, *IS*, no. 27.
c. inscription, Černy, *IS*, no. 409.
d. inscription, Černy, *IS*, no. 413.
e. stela, Tallet, in: *Studies Bourriau*, 939-945.

Literature: Vernus, *Surnom*, 72, no. 331; Franke, *Doss.*, 766 (a-d); Tallet, in: *Studies Bourriau*, 943.

Dating: 12th Dynasty / Amenemhet III

Dossier No. 234	*ḏḥwtj*
Mother: *nbt-pr ḏḥwtj-ḥtp* (b)	Father: *ḏḥwtj-ḥtp* (b)
Titles: *šmsw n jmj-r st* (a) *rḫ nswt, jmj-r st* *wdpw jrj jʿḥ* (b)	Wife:

a. stela, Cairo, CG 20065, Lange-Schäfer, *CCG* I, 80-81.
b. stela, London, BM EA 805, *HTBM* III, pl. 40.

[The title of his mother, *ḏḥwtj-ḥtp jrt.n ttt*, is attested on stela Louvre C 171]

Literature: Franke, *Doss.*, 779.

Dating: late 12th Dynasty

Dossier No. 235	*ḏḥwtj-htp*
Mother: *w3ḏ-k3w.s* (b, c)	Father:
Titles: *zẖ3w ꜥ nswt, zẖ3w hn* (a) *jmj-r ẖtmt* (b, c)	Wife:

a. objects from his burial; Kamal, *ASAE*, 3, 1902, 277-280; Coffins B5C, B7C; funerary bed, Rigault, Delange, *RdE* 60, 2009, 63-110, pls. VI-XIX.
b. depicted in tomb of Djehutihotep (no. 2) at Bersheh; Newberry, *El Berscheh I,* pl. XXVIII.
c. mentioned in the tomb of his brother *zp* (no. 3) at Bersheh; Griffith, Newberry, *El Bersheh II,* 28

[connection between a and b/c uncertain]

Literature: Willems, *Chests of Life*, 77-78.

Dating: Senusret II – Senusret III

Dossier No. 236	*ddj*
Mother:	Father:
Titles: *ẖrp nfrw, zẖ3w nswt* (b)	Wife:

a. seals (partly broken), Bard-Fattovich, *Harbor*, 233 (S06/5, S06/10), fig. 97 c, d.
b. inscribed box, Bard-Fattovich, *Harbor*, 238, figs. 99 and 100.

[based on the provenance]

Literature: Bard-Fattovich, *Harbor*, 233.

Dating: 12th Dynasty / 8th year of Amenemhat IV

Dossier No. 237	*ḏd-ptḥ dd.tw-snb*
Mother:	Father:
Titles: *wr mḏw šmꜥw* (a) *jmj-r nwt ṯꜣtj* (b, c) a. seal, UC 11361, MMA 22.1.318, Martin, *seals*, nos. 1776-1777 (no. 1777 found at Lisht). b. seal, Martin, *seals*, no. 1775 (found at the Uronari Fort). c. seal, Martin, *seals*, no. 1778 (with second name *dd.tw-snb*).	Wife:
Literature: Grajetzki, *Beamte*, 27-29 (I.30).	
Dating: 13th Dynasty	

Indexes

Locations

Titles

Name index